D1029629

Bill Gates

by Adam Woog

Lucent Books, San Diego, CA

Titles in the People in the News series include:
Bill Gates
Michael Jordan
Dominique Moceanu
The Rolling Stones
Steven Spielberg
Oprah Winfrey

Library of Congress Cataloging-in-Publication Data
Woog, Adam, 1953–
  Bill Gates / by Adam Woog.
     p. cm. — (People in the news series)
  Includes bibliographical references and index.
  Summary: A biography of Bill Gates including his childhood, his early work in computers, the founding of Microsoft and the expansion of the company, his private life, and future prospects.
  ISBN 1-56006-256-8 (lib. bdg. : alk. paper)
  1. Gates, Bill, 1955–   —Juvenile literature. 2. Businessmen— United States—Biography—Juvenile literature. 3. Microsoft Corporation—History—Juvenile literature. 4. Computer software industry—United States—History—Juvenile literature. [1. Gates, Bill, 1955–   . 2. Businessmen. 3. Microsoft Corporation—History. 4. Computer software industry.] I. Title. II. Series: People in the news (San Diego, Calif.)
  HD9696.C62G33795   1999
  338.7'610053'092—dc21
[B]   98-18162
                                                          CIP
                                                           AC

Table of Contents

Foreword

FAME AND CELEBRITY are alluring. People are drawn to those who walk in fame's spotlight, whether they are known for great accomplishments or for notorious deeds. The lives of the famous pique public interest and attract attention, perhaps because their experiences seem in some ways so different from, yet in other ways so similar to, our own.

Newspapers, magazines, and television regularly capitalize on this fascination with celebrity by running profiles of famous people. For example, television programs such as *Entertainment Tonight* devote all of their programming to stories about entertainment and entertainers. Magazines such as *People* fill their pages with stories of the private lives of famous people. Even newspapers, newsmagazines, and television news frequently delve into the lives of well-known personalities. Despite the number of articles and programs, few provide more than a superficial glimpse at their subjects.

Lucent's People in the News series offers young readers a deeper look into the lives of today's newsmakers, the influences that have shaped them, and the impact they have had in their fields of endeavor and on other people's lives. The subjects of the series hail from many disciplines and walks of life. They include authors, musicians, athletes, political leaders, entertainers, entrepreneurs, and others who have made a mark on modern life and who, in many cases, will continue to do so for years to come.

These biographies are more than factual chronicles. Each book emphasizes the contributions, accomplishments, or deeds that have brought fame or notoriety to the individual and shows how that person has influenced modern life. Authors portray their subjects in a realistic, unsentimental light. For example, Bill Gates—the cofounder and chief executive officer of the software giant Microsoft—has been instrumental in making personal computers the most vital tool of the modern age. Few dispute his business savvy, his perseverance, or his technical expertise, yet critics say he is ruthless in his dealings with competitors and driven more by his desire to maintain Microsoft's dominance in the computer industry than by an interest in furthering technology.

In these books, young readers will encounter inspiring stories about real people who achieved success despite enormous obstacles. Oprah Winfrey—the most powerful, most watched, and wealthiest woman on television today—spent the first six years of her life in the care of her grandparents while her unwed mother sought work and a better life elsewhere. Her adolescence was colored by promiscuity, pregnancy at age fourteen, rape, and sexual abuse.

Each author documents and supports his or her work with an array of primary and secondary source quotations taken from diaries, letters, speeches, and interviews. All quotes are footnoted to show readers exactly how and where biographers derive their information and provide guidance for further research. The quotations enliven the text by giving readers eyewitness views of the life and accomplishments of each person covered in the People in the News series.

In addition, each book in the series includes photographs, annotated bibliographies, timelines, and comprehensive indexes. For both the casual reader and the student researcher, the People in the News series offers insight into the lives of today's newsmakers—people who shape the way we live, work, and play in the modern age.

A Life Less Ordinary

There are two types of tech companies: Those where the guy in charge knows how to surf, and those where he depends on experts on the beach to guide him.

—Microsoft executive Nathan Myhrvold

IN SOME WAYS, Bill Gates is an ordinary person. He grew up in a close-knit and supportive family. He loves pastimes like games and movies, but is mostly focused on his business. He is middle-aged and married, the father of a child, and the owner of a large suburban house.

In other ways, Bill is highly unusual. As cofounder and chief executive officer of the software giant Microsoft, he is the single most powerful figure in the computer business. He is that industry's most easily recognizable face. Not coincidentally, he was a multimillionaire by age thirty and as of mid–1997 was the richest person in the world.

Gates has done much to make computers, especially personal computers, what they are today: commonplace tools that affect virtually every aspect of modern life. His power, fame, and wealth, meanwhile, give him enormous influence over the future of computing—and of life in general. Journalist John Seabrook writes, "[F]ar from being on the margin of society, Gates is now in a position to determine what society is like."[1]

Primitive Computing

When Bill was young, computing was a subject understood by just a handful of scientists. There were only a few hundred computers in the world, and the term "software" had not yet been introduced.

Bill was in college when he and a friend, Paul Allen, were attracted to a new development in this esoteric field: micro-computers. In later incarnations, these desktop-sized machines would come to be known as personal computers or PCs.

Most computer specialists thought that microcomputers would never be more than interesting toys for hobbyists. But Bill and Paul glimpsed their potential. They adapted the computer language called BASIC so that programs written in it could run on a specific microcomputer, the Altair, the world's first commercial microcomputer.

Today, the Altair seems hopelessly primitive compared with the simplest pocket calculator. Its arrival, however, marked the beginning of a revolution in the way the world sends, receives, stores, and handles information—and thus in the way modern society learns, plays, and works.

Information Revolution

A similarly dramatic shift in information technology came with the invention of movable type. Movable type and the printing press, which Johannes Gutenberg perfected in about 1450, made it possible to mass-produce books quickly and cheaply.

Before Gutenberg, about thirty thousand books existed in all of Europe. Each was handmade, and nearly all had religious themes. By 1500, only about fifty years after Gutenberg perfected his invention, there were over 9 million books in Europe, on a wide variety of

Bill Gates, cofounder and chief executive officer of software giant Microsoft, enjoys a relaxed moment in his office.

Bill Gates (right) and Paul Allen, who together formed Microsoft in 1975, stand before a board on which they have sketched some of the basic features of their revolutionary software product, the Windows operating system.

topics. Reading, once a skill possessed by only an elite few, began to be much more widely taught.

More recently, the world of computers has created such swift and profound changes that the present period is often called the Information Age. Computers are providing radical advances, with new opportunities opening up every day. They will, Bill Gates predicts in his book *The Road Ahead,* "transform our culture as dramatically as Gutenberg's press did the Middle Ages."[2]

Microsoft and the Information Age

In 1975, not long before Bill's twentieth birthday, Gates and Paul Allen formed a tiny company called Microsoft. Bill recalls thinking about the budding world of computing, "Maybe there was a place for the two of us."[3]

There was. Microsoft was perfectly poised to be at the center of the Information Age. The personal computer market exploded, and Microsoft grew with it. Through a combination of luck, hard work, technical know-how, and business sense, the company became the world's leading manufacturer of software.

Today, it is hard to imagine life without personal computers. Nearly half of all American homes now have them, and the figures are rising rapidly both in the United States and abroad. Roughly 90 percent of these machines rely on operating systems or other software from Microsoft. Bill's often-repeated slogan, "A computer on every desk and in every home, each one running Microsoft software," is coming closer to reality.

Drilling Down

Paul Allen is no longer active in Microsoft, although he retains stock in the company and sits on its board of directors. For years, Bill Gates has been the firm's chief executive officer, driving force, and very public symbol.

Part of Gates's public image stems from his formidable intellect. Virtually everyone who has had contact with him emphasizes that he is, without a doubt, the smartest person the speaker has ever met.

The saying at Microsoft headquarters in Redmond, Washington, (a suburb of Seattle), is that talking to most people is like sipping from a water fountain; talking to Bill is like drinking from a fire hose. People at Microsoft often speak of their boss in computer terms, describing his "incredible processing power." Or they may use network jargon like "unlimited bandwidth" to refer to his apparently endless capacity to handle data.

Equally famous is his intense focus, which lets him ignore everything but the problem at hand. In Microspeak, the slang used around Microsoft, this is known as getting hard-core or drilling down to the essentials.

Gates is well known for his ability to multitask—that is, to attend to several situations simultaneously without wasting time or making mistakes. In his office, for instance, he works on two computers. One has four frames that bring data from the Internet, while another is devoted to the hundreds of e-mail messages he sends and receives daily.

Bill craves a constant flow of information. According to one legend, he used to keep a map of Africa in his garage, with the idea of allowing his eyes to sweep it while he was getting in and out of his car, thus absorbing at least two mini-geography lessons a day. Tom Corddry, a former Microsoft executive, refers to the fabled riches brought to ancient warrior-kings with his remark that Bill is at the heart of "one of the information centers of the universe. It just flows into him at a tremendous rate, from all directions. If information were some kind of tribute, he'd be Kubla Khan."[4]

Personal Style

But Gates is not, by any means, simply a computer on two legs. He reads incessantly on a wide variety of subjects and can discuss at length a broad array of topics, both scientific and nonscientific.

He has a mischievous side, and he is a decent athlete. He loves water-skiing, and he occasionally shows off another athletic ability: jumping high from a standing or walking position. As a child, he amused his friends by hoisting himself into an empty garbage can and leaping out, landing cleanly on the ground. Walking in the halls at Microsoft, he will sometimes spontaneously leap and try to touch the ceiling.

Gates still retains other mannerisms of his youth. He peppers his speech with slang like "crummy," "neat," and "cool." He is quick to cut other people down with sarcasm, and the Microsoft employees who last the longest tend to be those who can, and will, stand up to him in shouting matches.

He is legendary, in fact, for his temper tantrums and willingness to shout others down during meetings. Some of the phrases hurled in these encounters—such as "That's the stupidest thing I've ever heard!"—have become part of Microsoft legend.

Although these days Gates usually appears publicly in crisp suits or preppy sports clothes, for most of his life he was indifferent to what he wore, whether his hair was combed, or whether he had recently showered. This is still true to an extent. Esther Dyson, an influential computer journalist who has known Gates well for many years, remarks: "I'm told that within Microsoft certain people are allowed to take Bill's glasses off and wipe them, but I've never done it. You know, it's like— 'Don't try this at home.'"[5]

Gates after announcing the release of Windows 95, a major product upgrade, at Microsoft headquarters in Redmond, Washington, in August 1995.

Genius?

Because of his ability to process information, Gates has sometimes been called a genius. He himself prefers terms like "supersmart," his description of the kind of people he likes to hire.

Many observers, however, feel that his success is due to personality factors that have little to do with pure intelligence.

He is, for one thing, a brilliant businessman, and has consistently made canny moves to outdistance the competition. In this regard, he has been compared to Thomas Edison, a technical wizard who also triumphed as a business entrepreneur.

Gates himself discounts the business side of his life, often stating that business "isn't that complicated" and estimating that only about 10 percent of his thinking is devoted to business. "If you're any good at math at all, you understand business," he says. "It's not its own deep, deep subject."[6]

Bill's business savvy, meanwhile, is combined with a relentless drive to win, an attitude nurtured when he was a boy, playing games with his fiercely competitive family.

The need to win has not won Gates many friends in the industry. His critics say that he tries to smash rivals, like oil baron John D. Rockefeller and other tycoons who ruthlessly destroyed their competitors. "Competing with Bill Gates," says a one-time business rival, former Lotus Software chairman Mitch Kapor, "is like putting your head in a vise and turning the handle. He doesn't take no for an answer, and he keeps coming back."[7]

Perhaps the key to Gates's success is his ability to combine business savvy and a relentless pursuit of winning with a third trait: superb technical knowledge. Most executives of software companies are professional managers or technical wizards, but not both. Few are as knowledgeable as Bill about all sides of a particular undertaking. Journalist Fred Moody remarks, "Gates' ability to leap agilely from the technical details of any given project to its business case and back again is most often cited as the attribute setting him apart from everyone else in his industry."[8]

The Great Adventure

Some critics maintain that Gates is less interested in furthering technology than in maintaining Microsoft's dominance. They worry that too much power—indeed, the future direction of the Information Age—is in the hands of one man. One rival software executive, acknowledging that nice guys don't always win, remarks,

> Bill believes that now is not the time for statesmanship. Now is the time to conquer new foes, plunder new lands. . . . You know, Mother Teresa is not going to build the broadband network of the future.[9]

For better or worse, Bill Gates is at the heart of the Information Age. A longtime friend, computer entrepreneur Ann Winblad, remarks, "[W]e began a great adventure on the fringes of a little-known industry and it landed us at the center of an amazing universe."[10]

That great adventure, for Bill, began in Seattle, Washington, in 1955.

Chapter 1

Childhood

*We all knew Bill was smarter than us. Even back then, when
he was nine or ten years old, he talked like an adult and could
express himself in ways none of us understood.*
—a childhood friend of Bill Gates

SEATTLE IN THE 1950s was a pleasant, small Pacific Northwest
city. Its surrounding terrain of mountains, lakes, and salt water
shaped its main economic activities: fishing and timber. The
biggest single industry was the production of aircraft at the Boeing Company. People who lived in Seattle tended to favor out-
door activities, and the atmosphere was relatively relaxed.

Within this world—neither small town nor booming
metropolis—the Gates family was well known.

The Gates Family

Both of Bill's parents could trace their Northwest roots to the late
1800s, when the area was first settled by white homesteaders.

Bill Senior (as he is now usually known) grew up in nearby
Bremerton, the son of a prosperous local merchant. He served
in World War II, attended law school at the University of Washington, and was the city attorney for Bremerton before going
into private practice in Seattle.

In 1951 Bill Senior married Mary Higgins, whom he had
met when they were both students. An energetic and high-
spirited outdoorswoman, active in sororities and student government, Mary became a schoolteacher after graduation. Like
Bill Senior, she came from a well-to-do local family; her grand-
father had been a banker. The couple's first child, Kristianne,

Downtown Seattle, Washington, Gates's hometown. Later, young Bill would enjoy a similar view after winning a dinner at the restaurant atop the city's Space Needle.

was born in 1953. Two years later, on October 28, 1955, William Henry Gates III was born at Swedish Hospital.

Rocking Baby

Bill's maternal grandmother, who loved playing cards, nicknamed the boy Trey (pronounced "tray")—a card-playing term for "three"—to distinguish him from the other Bills in the family. The name stuck, and Microsoft's chief executive is still known to his family as Trey.

As a baby, Bill displayed one of the personal quirks that would become famous in later years. He rocked on a rocking horse and in his cradle constantly, a trait that has stayed with him into adulthood. He is well known for rocking rhythmically while thinking or speaking. Gates says about his rocking:

> I think it's just excess energy. I should stop, but I haven't yet. They claim I started at an extremely young age. I had a rocking horse and they used to put me to sleep on my rocking horse, and I think that addicted me.[11]

As a boy he was small and skinny and energetic, with a high-pitched voice, big feet, and a clumsy manner. Bill also had no apparent fashion sense. He didn't care how sloppily he dressed or how many days he'd worn a shirt.

"Think Smart!"

The Gates family loved competitive games like Password and trivia contests. "The play was quite serious," Bill Senior recalls. "Winning mattered."[12]

The family also held lively dinnertime conversations about a wide variety of topics. In later interviews, Bill has often remarked on how lucky he was to have such a close-knit and intellectually rich early environment.

As the years went on, Bill Senior became increasingly busy. Mary, meanwhile, was more and more active in local causes and serving on the boards of various organizations. As a result, Mary's mother, Adelle Maxwell, often took care of the children in the afternoons.

Three-and-a-half-year-old Bill and his mother, Mary. Once a schoolteacher, she often gave lectures to Seattle-area schools and participated in many other volunteer activities.

Trey and Kristianne affectionately called their grandmother Gam. Like the rest of the family, Gam loved highly competitive games, especially bridge. She saw game playing as a good test of skill and intelligence, and her appreciation of these qualities had an enormous impact on Bill's later life. Mary Gates once recalled, "She was always saying to him, 'Think smart! Think smart!'"[13]

Hangman

The Gates family's gamesmanship extended even to important announcements. Bill Senior and Mary broke the news of Mary's third pregnancy to Trey and Kristianne by giving them a message encoded in a game of hangman: "A little visitor is coming soon." The second Gates daughter, Libby, was born in 1964.

Summers for the Gates family were spent outdoors, water-skiing and swimming at the Laurelhurst Beach Club. They also spent long weeks at Cheerio, a rustic collection of cabins shared by several families on nearby Hood Canal.

The families organized nightly campfires and skits, as well as tennis tournaments and other daylight sports activities. High-lighting these summer months were the weekly Cheerio Olympics, elaborately detailed games that combined intellectual and physical activity. They fueled even further the Gates family's love of spirited horseplay and competition.

Smart Kid

When Bill was in grade school, his parents more than once considered holding him back because of his small size. However, teachers at View Ridge Elementary convinced the Gateses that their son was more than capable of staying with his age level.

When Bill was in the fourth grade, the family moved to a house in Laurelhurst, an upper-middle-class neighborhood on the edge of Lake Washington and near the University of Washington. Bill started at a new school, Laurelhurst Elementary.

It was always clear that Bill was bright and interested in more than just math and science. He loved classic kids' books like *Charlotte's Web* and *Doctor Doolittle*. By age nine he had read the entire *World Book* encyclopedia. He also helped the school librarian track lost books, after regular library hours.

Bill was a precocious workaholic—previewing the eighty-hour weeks he would routinely put in at Microsoft. Assigned to write a report on the human body during a one-hour period, Bill wrote fourteen pages; most of his classmates had turned in a single page. Childhood friend Carl Edmark says, "Everything Bill did, he did to the max. What he did always went well, well beyond everyone else."[14]

World's Fair

Throughout grade school, Bill did poorly in penmanship, citizenship, and other subjects he found trivial—but he got top grades in science and math. His interest in the sciences was cemented in 1962, when Seattle hosted a World's Fair that emphasized technology and the future.

Among the displays was a Univac mainframe computer, which took up an entire room. There were also such breathtaking novelties as large-screen color TVs and movies that could be shown immediately after being shot—that is, video. Bill was interested in the fair's roller coaster, but he was entranced by the technology.

He also showed a remarkable ability for both quick memorization and deep understanding. When he was eleven, this

The Little Emperor

From a very early age, Bill Gates has been fascinated by the story of Napoleon, whose life seems to resonate with Gates's own hopes, ambitions, and will. In *Gates,* journalists Steve Manes and Paul Andrews quote their subject:

How can an ugly little guy who isn't even really French manage to rise up and rewrite the laws of Europe so that even today the Code Napoleon is a big thing? And the way he recognized scientific and artistic leaders of the time: That's a pretty unusual thing. . . .

At a time when there was no opportunity for leadership, most leaders were killed or overthrown, [Napoleon] put himself into such an incredible position and yet ruined his own success. The thing that's incredible about it is that at the end of his life he sat on an island and he dictated his thoughts. This is one smart guy.

Crowds line up to visit one of the many exhibits at the Seattle World's Fair in 1962. The Fair was host to many technological breakthroughs, including powerful computers which enthralled the young Gates.

combination won Bill a dinner at the revolving restaurant atop Seattle's Space Needle.

The Reverend Dale Turner, pastor of the family's church, University Congregational, had promised the dinner to any young person who could memorize the Sermon on the Mount, a biblical passage over two thousand words long. Turner recalls:

> I needed only to go to his home that day to know that he was something special. I couldn't imagine how an 11-year-old boy could have a mind like that. And my subsequent questioning of him revealed a deep understanding of the passage.[15]

Contracts

Throughout his youth, Bill excelled at some sports despite his small build. He was especially good at tennis and water-skiing. He was also active in Boy Scouts; his father had been an Eagle Scout. Although Bill never acquired the right badges to make the same rank, he did achieve a life ranking just short of Eagle.

In both fourth and fifth grades, Bill listed "scientist" as the occupation he wanted to pursue. However, even in grade school he was also showing a keen interest in business. For example, for one sixth-grade economics unit Bill wrote a detailed mock business proposal called "Invest with Gatesway," in which he imagined himself an entrepreneur starting a medical care company.

Bill also demonstrated an appreciation for tough negotiations at a young age, a trait perhaps nurtured by his lawyer father. In 1966 Bill wrote his first contract. It stated that in return for $5 "on acceptance of terms," Bill would receive unlimited, nonexclusive rights to his sister's baseball glove. "When Trey wants the mitt, he gets it."[16]

Problem Kid

Toward the end of his elementary years, Bill started having some behavioral problems that worried his parents and teachers.

He seemed emotionally immature, overly talkative, and far too sarcastic. His desk at school was always messy. His room at home was such a disaster that his mother had stopped going into it; she asked only that Bill keep his door shut so she couldn't see the mess.

Bill's withering sarcasm, always one of his least attractive traits, was directed at the world in general. An incident from Bill's sixth-grade year illustrates this. When his mother called him to dinner from his basement bedroom, he wouldn't respond.

> "What are you doing?" she demanded over the intercom.
> "I'm thinking," he shouted back.
> "You're thinking?"
> "Yes, Mom, I'm thinking," he said sarcastically. "Have you ever tried thinking?"[17]

Bill's problems at school grew serious enough to prompt his parents to send him to a psychiatrist. Bill says he now regards this brief experience as an opportunity to explore someone else's knowledge and expand his own mind:

> [The psychiatrist] said some profound things that got me thinking a little differently. He was a cool guy. . . . I only saw him for a year and a half, and never saw him again,

and I haven't been to anybody like that ever since. But my mind was focused appropriately.[18]

Lakeside

The elder Gateses hoped that some of their son's problems could be corrected. At the same time, they did not want to stifle Bill's budding intellect and curiosity. Thus they decided to send him to a private, all-boys school starting with seventh grade. "We became concerned about him when he was ready for junior high," Bill Senior recalls. "He was so small and shy, in need of protection, and his interests were so very different from the typical sixth grader's."[19]

The Lakeside School is a prestigious private institution, situated on a quiet campus resembling that of a small New England school. It is competitive and academic, and many of its graduates have gone on to become important leaders in the Pacific Northwest and beyond.

Bill entered the seventh grade at Lakeside in 1967.

He encountered there both a person and a machine that would help set his future course. The person was a student named Paul Allen, and the machine was a Teletype, which was hooked up to a primitive mainframe computer.

Chapter 2

Discovering Computers

Anyone who remembers him as a nerdy person either didn't deal with him closely or is remembering wrong.
                          —high school friend Paul Carlson

LAKESIDE WAS IN many ways a typical boys' school. It loosened up somewhat during the era of Vietnam and student protests, but uniforms, neat hair, and strict rules were the order of the day.

Lakeside was also the most exclusive of the area's schools, attracting the best and the brightest. As a classmate of Bill's puts it, "Even the dumb kids were smart."[20]

Bill's behavioral problems subsided in this atmosphere. Perhaps this was because he was now more challenged intellectually by his classmates and teachers. Nonetheless, he did not excel overall, because he still gave little attention to subjects that bored him. Throughout junior high and high school, he maintained a B average, with A's in math making up for poorer grades in other subjects.

Teletype

At the beginning of eighth grade in 1968 Bill returned to Lakeside to discover something new.

The Lakeside Rummage Sale is a huge event that raises thousands of dollars for the school every year. In 1968 the school spent some of this money on equipment to help students explore a new and largely unknown world: computing. The purchases included a teletypewriter similar to those machines found in newsrooms; its gear included a keyboard, a device for "reading" punched-paper tape, and an acoustic modem.

The school's new set of hardware lacked a CPU, or central processing unit. Instead, the acoustic modem, which was connected to a telephone handset, linked the Lakeside equipment to a huge mainframe computer, and time on the mainframe was sold on an hourly basis. By today's standards the setup was clumsy and crude. In 1968, however, it was exciting and unusual for a school to own such hardware.

An informal group of Lakeside students quickly formed around the new equipment. They didn't know much about it, but they were entranced and began skipping classes to spend more time with the machine. Skipping was so common that the chairman of the math department invented the log-on password GYMFLAKE, a reference to those who flaked out of gym class in favor of computing.

"The Kids Could Control It"

From the beginning, Bill was one of the best at understanding the new machine. Bill Dougall, a math teacher who was one of the Lakeside faculty members in charge of the computer, recalls, "I go around saying I taught him all he knows. It took him a week to pass me."[21]

In the early days of computing, prepackaged software and sophisticated operating systems did not exist. Even the simplest

"Some Toy"

In this passage from *The Road Ahead*, Bill Gates reflects on his early infatuation with computers and software.

Like all kids, we not only fooled around with our toys, we changed them. If you've ever watched a child with a cardboard carton and a box of crayons create a spaceship with cool control panels, or listened to their improvised rules, such as "Red cars can jump all others," then you know that this impulse to make a toy do more is at the heart of innovative childhood play. It is also the essence of creativity.

Of course, in those days we were just goofing around, or so we thought. But the toy we had—well, it turned out to be some toy. . . . School kids today are doing amazing things with personal computers that are no larger than textbooks but outperform the largest computers of a generation ago.

Bill watches Paul Allen at the keyboard of Lakeside School's teletypewriter. Purchased with money raised at a school rummage sale, the equipment introduced the pair to the new and entrancing world of computing, one which Bill easily mastered.

command to a computer had to be written, or programmed, by the user in a language that would be accepted by the mainframe. The most common programming language was BASIC, short for Beginner's All-purpose Symbolic Instruction Code. It was designed for use by people who were not computer professionals. This was the language that Bill and the other kids learned.

The first program Bill wrote made the computer do simple mathematical conversions, changing a number from one arithmetic base to another. His second program let a human play tic-tac-toe with the computer.

As he recalls in *The Road Ahead,* the mainframe was "huge and cumbersome and slow and absolutely compelling." It might take an entire lunch period for the machine to work its way through a single game of tic-tac-toe: "But who cared? There was just something neat about the machine. I realized later part of the appeal was that here was an enormous, expensive, grown-up machine and we, the kids, could control it."[22]

Clients of the Digital Equipment Corporation review printouts from the state-of-the-art PDP-10 computer. Bill and other Lakeside students spent hours "debugging" machines such as this one in exchange for free computer time.

C Cubed

The big problem was time. Renting time on the mainframe was expensive. The students soon used up their entire year's budget.

Help came from a new company in Seattle: Computer Center Corporation, or C Cubed (C x C x C=C^3). Its owners bought a mainframe computer and planned to rent time to clients such as Boeing.

In a former car showroom, C Cubed installed a computer, a Digital Equipment Corporation model PDP-10. The PDP-10 was the size of a refrigerator, cost millions of dollars, and required an air-conditioned room. Even with constant maintenance, it crashed every half-hour or so. Still, it was a state-of-the-art machine; its disk drive had a then-staggering 8 megabytes of storage.

In the early days of commercial computing, companies such as Digital Equipment often sold their machines on a trial basis, an arrangement that gave clients a chance to discover faults and advise the vendor, which was then under the gun to correct them. The people at C Cubed needed to work the machine hard to uncover its bugs early on, before the trial period had ended, and with it Digital's offer to fix the bugs at no charge.

Someone at C Cubed proposed that the eager kids at Lakeside would be perfect bug-catchers. Their pay would be free computer time. For the Lakesiders, it was heaven.

Hacking

The students came into the C Cubed offices on Saturday mornings to work on the teletype units connected to the mainframe. Soon they were there after school too.

Bill would sometimes also steal out at night and take the bus to the C Cubed offices. "Trey got so into it," his father recalls, "that he would sneak out the basement door after we went to bed and spend most of the night there."[23] Mary Gates wondered why it was hard for Bill to get up early on some mornings.

Eventually, the Lakesiders used up their free time at C Cubed. They decided to take matters into their own hands. Someone—to this day, no one admits to knowing who—hacked into the system, accessing accounts and giving the Lakesiders more time.

Today, hacking into a private computer network is against the law. At that time, however, it was considered more simple mischief than a criminal act. Circumventing a supposedly secure system, after all, uncovered its weaknesses. Dick Gruen, a programmer at C Cubed, remarks, "I would not call it breaking in if I said, 'See if you can find a way around this.' I'd call it asking people to see whether the watchman was doing his job."[24]

Still, the Massachusetts company that manufactured the computer was not happy to learn what the Lakesiders had done. It created a harder code, which the Lakesiders cracked in about an hour and a half. The students then showed the adults how they had done it.

In the early 1970s the Seattle area experienced a severe economic depression, and many people lost their jobs and businesses. One of the casualties was C Cubed.

When the company went bankrupt, the Lakesiders saved their work by downloading files onto tape. They did this as the repossession firm was hauling away the office furniture. When all the chairs were gone, they finished the job on their knees.

LPG

In 1970, the students who were most serious about computing—Bill Gates, Paul Allen, Kent Evans, and Ric Weiland—banded together as the Lakeside Programmers Group in an effort to get jobs.

The group, LPG for short, was not without conflict. At one point, Bill and Kent bought some blank paper tapes, the primitive storage medium now superseded by floppy disks and CD-ROMs. They tried to keep the purchase secret from Paul and Ric, but Paul found out and stole the tapes. This led to a furious argument, but eventually the four agreed to keep some of the tapes and sell the rest at a profit.

The members of LPG got their first shot at "real" computing when a company in Portland, Oregon, hired them to create a payroll program in exchange for the experience—that is, free computer time. The challenge was that the code had to be written in COBOL (COmmon Business-Oriented Language). COBOL was the standard language for most businesses, but the students had to learn it from scratch to complete the project.

In the fall, Paul and Ric went off to college. Paul attended nearby Washington State University, and Ric headed to California and Stanford. Kent and Bill, two years younger, remained at Lakeside.

Many people who knew Kent and Bill as high school students have commented that Bill's interest in business was strongly influenced by his friend Kent, the son of a minister. "We read *Fortune* together; we were going to conquer the world," Gates recalls. "I still remember his phone number."[25]

Scheduling

That same fall, Lakeside merged with a private girls' school, St. Nicholas. Scheduling classes for the newly enlarged school was a nightmare, made worse because many girls were splitting their time between the Lakeside campus and that of St. Nicholas, ten miles away.

One Lakeside teacher had tried to computerize the scheduling, but with limited success. When the teacher was killed in an accident, the school asked Bill and Kent to try.

The two were wary, knowing how difficult it would be to satisfy everyone. But Lakeside offered to pay them, and they eventually embarked on a tough regimen of programming in addition to their regular studies.

Then, in May 1972, another tragedy struck. Partly to relieve the stress of the scheduling project, Kent had enrolled in a mountaineering course that offered practical experience in this potentially dangerous pursuit. On a hike with the class, Kent lost his footing and fell hundreds of feet down a glacier; he died aboard the rescue helicopter.

Everyone who knew Kent Evans, including Bill, was devastated. "I had never thought of people dying," Bill recalls. "At the service, I was supposed to speak, but I couldn't get up. For two weeks I couldn't do anything at all."[26]

Despite his grief, Bill had to finish the project. He turned to Paul Allen, back in Seattle for the summer from Washington State University. Together they finished the program.

According to legend, Bill and Paul made sure that the daughter of the headmaster got exactly the schedule she wanted. Legend also says that Bill created a history class with only one other boy in it besides himself, even though the overall boy/girl ratio was three to one.

Traf-0-Data

As Bill's senior year at Lakeside began, he started reading in electronics magazines about a new device, Intel's 8080 microchip. The 8080 was the first programmable chip; in other words, instead

Intel's 8080 programmable microchip. The revolutionary chip inspired Bill and Paul to build their own computer for their first company, called Traf-0-Data.

A Lakeside yearbook photo of Gates in the school's computer room.

of being limited to performing only one task, as with "hard-wired" microchips, it could do many tasks in sequence depending on the software.

The potential for the practical use of a programmable microchip was immense. Bill writes in his book *The Road Ahead* that a microprocessor capable of doing only one application is like a musical instrument in the hands of an amateur: "A powerful microprocessor with programming languages, however, is like an accomplished orchestra. With the right software, or sheet music, it can play anything."[27]

Bill and Paul decided they would build their own computer around the new chip, to make it "play" the way they wanted it to. They had an idea to make a machine for a specific purpose: processing data about traffic patterns obtained from car-counting boxes—devices attached to hoses that lay across roadways and relayed a signal when a vehicle drove over.

Bill had already worked on a program to do this for a Seattle software company, but he thought he could improve on the design. To implement the plan, Bill and Paul bought a chip for $360 and enlisted the help of a friend, Paul Gilbert, a wizard with hardware, who later became a partner, as well.

Thus was born Traf-O-Data, Bill and Paul's first company. Traf-O-Data was never a success, but it gave the partners valuable experience in computing and in business.

From the beginning, the company was plagued with problems. One night, the prototype system crashed repeatedly while Bill was demonstrating it to a city official in the Gates family living room. Bill finally had to plead with his mother to tell the official that it really had worked the night before.

TRW

Later that year, Bill and Paul got jobs with the giant aerospace company TRW.

TRW had a contract to operate the Bonneville Power Authority's hydroelectric facility in Vancouver, Washington. (This small town in the southwestern part of Washington State should not be confused with Vancouver, Canada.)

A system was needed to help monitor the flow of electricity from hydroelectric plants along the Columbia River. The project was behind schedule and more complex than anyone had imagined; TRW was desperate for help.

Bill and Paul agreed to work for $4 an hour. It was a ridiculously low sum for seasoned programmers, but it was fair enough for a high school senior working on a class project—which is how Bill justified the time-consuming affair to his teachers and parents.

In the spring of 1973, Bill resumed life at Lakeside. He acted in school plays, won a National Merit scholarship, graduated, and was accepted by all three of his top university choices. This was expected; Bill had scored a perfect 800 in math and in the low 700s on the verbals on his Scholastic Aptitude Test (SAT). Sending regrets to Princeton and Yale, he accepted the offer from Harvard.

Tang from the Jar

Bill and Paul then returned to Vancouver for the summer. Ric Weiland came along as well, and the three roomed together in a small apartment. Not that they spent much time there; the trio was famous for all-night programming sessions and rarely went home even to bathe. They more or less camped out at the TRW offices and

Fearless

Bill Gates Senior, quoted in Manes and Andrews's book *Gates,* reflects on the strong impression made on his son by his friend Kent Evans.

> Most kids grow up mostly being told about all the things that you're too young to do: "You can't do that, you couldn't possibly do that." Somehow that never was ever any influence in Kent's life, because he didn't see any limits. . . . He was fearless. . . . He'd do anything. He'd just pick up the phone and call people. He just didn't have any sense of inhibition or limit about what he could do because he was a fifteen-year-old or whatever he was at the time. . . . I don't know how much of that is natural to [Bill] and how much he got from the influence of Kent.

survived on pizza and Instant Tang, scooped out of the jar and eaten with a spoon. (The manufacturer's instructions were to add water to the orange granules and drink the juicelike beverage that resulted.)

When taking a break, Bill and Paul would work on their Traf-O-Data project or play games. Bill was better at Go, but Paul would usually win at chess. Bill was known to occasionally upset the table "by accident" if he was close to losing.

The TRW experience was valuable in both positive and negative ways. Bill and Paul had the satisfaction of successfully completing a large project, and they gained experience working with some of the top computer engineers in the country.

On the other hand, TRW unwittingly taught them how *not* to run a large-scale operation. The massive corporation thought problems could be solved simply by applying more manpower and spending more money. Bill was probably referring to this approach when he remarked,

> Before Paul and I started [Microsoft], we had been involved in some large-scale software projects that were real disasters. They just kept pouring people in, and nobody really knew how they were going to stabilize the project. We swore to ourselves that we would do better.[28]

For years, Bill had been telling people that he was going to make a million dollars by the time he was twenty. As he prepared to leave for Harvard, that age—and that prediction—grew closer.

Chapter 3

Writing BASIC

I'd have to say BASIC for the 8080, because of the effect it's had, and because of how appropriate it was at the time, and because we managed to get it so small.
　　　　　—Bill Gates, when asked to name his greatest
　　　　　　　　　　　　achievement in programming

IN THE FALL OF 1973, the members of the Lakeside Programmers Group went their separate ways. Paul returned to WSU, Ric went back to Stanford, and Bill left for Harvard University in Cambridge, Massachusetts.

Rude Awakening

Bill's official major at Harvard was applied math. His first classes, however, were a rude awakening.

He had always been the best math student in his classes, and over the years had become arrogant about his abilities. Now for the first time he encountered people who were as gifted, or more so, than himself. "It kind of confused me that there were people who actually were better at math than me," he recalls, using a scientific term to add: "It was a new data point."[29]

He held his own but did not excel in his other classes, which included Greek literature, social science, English history, and organic chemistry. Bill scorned Harvard's computer classes as too simple; he already knew more than many of the professors—or at least thought he did. He recalls:

> I was a little bit insufferable. I took this very advanced computer class and there were all these graduate students in computer science. I would sit there and wait

until they all agreed on something stupid and then, in a very sarcastic way, I'd tell them that they were wrong.[30]

Bill began his own informal computer studies and was a regular at Harvard's computer center, the Aiken Computational Laboratory. The freshman soon was using machines normally reserved for upperclassmen and graduate students. The director of the Aiken Lab, Thomas Cheatham, recalls that the young prodigy offset his gifts with less attractive qualities: "He was a hell of a good programmer [but] he's an obnoxious human being. . . . He'd put people down when it was not necessary, and just generally not be a pleasant fellow to have around the place."[31]

The College Life

Bill's personal habits were likewise not to everyone's taste. He was well known for not bothering to bathe or wash his hair. He did his laundry as infrequently as possible and reportedly neglected to use sheets on his bed.

Generally, Bill was indifferent to the major pastimes of many college students, such as music. He did have a few Jimi Hendrix albums pushed on him by Paul Allen, who idolized the Seattle-born guitarist. By all accounts, however, he was not very interested in the opposite sex, either. His roommate, Sam Znaimer, recalls, "[T]he rest of us were more overwhelmed by our hormones than Bill. I don't remember him chasing any women, and there were lots of opportunities."[32]

Bill's work habits consisted of staying up all night and surviving on hamburgers and pizza. This lifestyle may have contributed to the serious digestive illness he contracted at the end of his freshman year, while studying for finals. The disease, called ulcerative colitis, is often genetic, but it can be triggered by stress, overwork, and bad diet.

After a week in the hospital, Bill flew home to recuperate over the summer. He thought about taking a year off and interviewed with several computer companies, but ended up returning to Harvard in the fall.

For his sophomore year, Bill moved into Currier House, a coed dorm filled with science students. His academic strategy was to sign up for courses he knew would be easy for him and

The "Poker Room" at Currier House on the Harvard campus, where Bill spent many nights playing cards.

then audit others—that is, attend the classes without registering for them. This ensured he would get good grades while "secretly" studying the things that most interested him.

Typically, he ignored the easy subjects until final exam time. Then he would quickly cram to pass the test. In *The Road Ahead,* Bill writes:

> In college there is a lot of posturing, and appearing to slack off was considered a great way to establish your coolness. Therefore . . . I instituted a deliberate policy of skipping most classes and then studying feverishly at the end of the term. It became a game . . . to see how high a grade I could pull while investing the least time possible.[33]

If a subject did grab his attention, Bill could apply the remarkable concentration that was already a familiar characteristic. He could focus so closely that nothing distracted him. "He was able to block out all the external noise," Sam Znaimer recalls.[34]

Not all Bill's interests lay in math and computers. For instance, he devoured books about people he admired. "I've read more about Napoleon than anyone else," Bill says, "and I've read everything I can about [Leonardo] da Vinci and Franklin Roosevelt."[35]

Friends

During his first year at Harvard, Bill had remained in close touch with Paul Allen. Now Paul was living nearby.

Having grown bored with eastern Washington, where WSU is located, Paul had accepted a job at Honeywell, a large electronics company in Boston—a stone's throw from Bill.

Down the hall at Currier House, meanwhile, was a hearty student from Detroit named Steve Ballmer. Despite their outward differences—unlike Bill, Steve was huge and extroverted—the two became pals. They shared a similar taste in movies, a cynical sense of humor, and an aptitude for math. Steve encouraged Bill to be more outgoing, persuading him to undertake ventures such as joining one of Harvard's eating clubs and exploring city nightlife. It was the beginning of a relationship that would intensify years later, when Steve became a crucial part of the Microsoft team.

At Currier, Bill increasingly indulged his love of games. In particular, he began taking part in all-night poker sessions. Steve Ballmer recalls, "He'd play poker until 6 in the morning, then I'd run into him at breakfast and discuss applied mathematics. . . . He was eccentric but charismatic."[36]

He was also obsessed with the first video games, which today seem hopelessly slow and old-fashioned but were then exciting entertainment. Bill especially loved Pong, a form of Ping-Pong, as well as a game called Breakout. Ironically, Breakout was designed by two people who became important to Bill in later years: Steve Jobs and Steve Wozniak, the cofounders of Apple Computer.

"PROJECT BREAKTHROUGH!"

In December 1974 Paul Allen bought a magazine at a newsstand in Harvard Square. It was the January 1975 issue of *Popular Electronics*, a periodical aimed at electronics hobbyists.

The cover photo showed an odd-looking blue box with thirty-six lights and twenty-five toggle switches. It looked like it had come from an Army-Navy surplus store. It had neither a keyboard nor a monitor.

"PROJECT BREAKTHROUGH!" the magazine's headline trumpeted. "World's First Minicomputer Kit to Rival Commercial Models. . . . Altair 8800 SAVE OVER $1000." The first sentence of the accompanying article was enthusiastic: "The era of the computer in every home—a favorite topic among science fiction writers—has arrived!"[37]

The Altair was not, strictly speaking, the first personal computer. In the 1950s, IBM had developed a prototype that was the size of a large desk, designed for one-person operation. Other early machines, such as Digital's PDP-8 (a smaller version of the PDP-10 used by Bill and his friends at Lakeside), could also be operated by a single person.

But none of these machines had been marketed to the public, and all were very expensive. The Altair was the first affordable, commercially available personal computer.

The Altair 8800 personal computer. Gates and Paul Allen contracted with its inventors to write BASIC programming that would enhance the machine's abilities and performance.

MITS

The company that made the Altair was located in Albuquerque, New Mexico. Micro Instrumentation and Telemetry Systems (MITS) had built its reputation on kits for calculators and radio transmitters for model rockets. Then its cofounders, Ed Roberts and Bill Yates, decided to design a computer based around Intel's 8080 microchip. The 8080 was the newest microchip available, with memory comprising a then-impressive 64Kbit of ROM and 256 bytes (not megabytes) of RAM.

For $397, computer hobbyists received a box full of toggles, ribbon cables, LED lights, mounting boards, capacitors, and other pieces. For $101, the company would assemble the parts.

Programming the Altair required hours of painstaking work, inputting sequences of instructions by flipping toggle switches. If any one of hundreds of commands was done incorrectly, the machine would shut down.

Even if the programmer managed to avoid all errors in setting the switches, all the machine could do was blink its lights on and off in sequence.

And yet the Altair was a hit—a far bigger one than Roberts and Yates had planned on. Their original sales estimate of two hundred machines a year proved extremely low. Computer hobbyists across the country had been waiting for just such a machine, and almost immediately demand far outstripped MITS's ability to maintain a supply. The company was soon overwhelmed with back orders.

Paul and Bill were among those enthralled by the Altair. Bill recalls, "[W]e thought, 'Geez, we'd better get going, because we know these machines are going to be popular.'"[38]

Double Bluff

The big drawback to the Altair, Bill and Paul saw, was that it had no language. They could not talk to it as they could with mainframe computers. They immediately began a plan to change that.

They figured that a version of BASIC for the Altair would radically alter its capabilities. They knew they could write one, but they also knew that others would have the same idea. They needed a head start, which they thought they could get by adapting a program they had developed for Traf-O-Data.

In a letter, the pair told Roberts that they had written a version of BASIC that would run on the Altair. The statement was a definite misrepresentation of the facts, but Roberts was interested. He needed software to make his machine usable, and he liked BASIC.

Bill and Paul had written the letter on Traf-O-Data stationery. When Roberts called the number on the letterhead, he got the home of the third Traf-O-Data partner, Paul Gilbert. Paul's mother politely told Roberts that she had no idea what he was talking about, and things nearly ended there.

Fortunately, Paul and Bill followed up with a phone call. Bill placed the call but identified himself as Paul Allen. This deception was based on the assumption that Paul would likely be the first to meet Roberts in person, because he looked more mature.

What followed was a mutual game of delay. Bill repeated the bluff that he already had a version of BASIC that would

Ed Roberts, codesigner of the Altair. At first, neither he nor Gates was sufficiently prepared to make improvements to the 8800, a project which would require marathon hours of writing new program code and fixing the computer's initial deficiencies.

work on the Altair. Roberts, meanwhile, knew that the reality of the Altair's usability was quite different from the rosy picture painted by the *Popular Electronics* article. It still needed work before it could handle BASIC.

Roberts therefore made a misleading statement of his own: He said he didn't have adequate memory cards for the machine. He asked for a month's delay before demonstrations were held. Bill, of course, agreed, since he still hadn't written the program. Paul recalls, "So we hung up the phone and Bill was sort of jubilant about this, and Bill says, 'God, we gotta get going on this!'"[39]

Getting Hard-Core

Bill and Paul were so sure of their ability to fulfill their end of the agreement in a month that they didn't even bother asking for an Altair kit. Instead, they located some programming manuals for the 8080 chip and got to work.

Paul concentrated on modifying the simulator he had developed for Traf-O-Data. He had to adapt a simulator that ran on the 8008 chip to one for the more powerful 8080.

Bill worked on the BASIC program itself, that is, the lines of code converting a 1960s version of BASIC into one that would work with the Altair. As a base, he borrowed Digital Equipment Corporation's version of the language. In the early days of computing, this practice was common; in fact, DEC's version had been built on still earlier programs developed elsewhere. The issue of copyright ownership would become important only in later years.

The first draft of Bill's program was written in about three and a half weeks of round-the-clock activity while he was still enrolled in Harvard. During these marathon sessions, his work habits became even more pronounced and, to use a phrase Bill made commonplace later, extremely hard-core. He often slept on the floor of Aiken Lab. Sometimes he fell asleep at the keyboard, then woke up and immediately started typing again.

Bill worked hard to make the code as lean as possible, so that it would require a minimum of the Altair's precious memory. Still, the finished program needed another 6Kbit of ROM—more memory than on any existing microcomputer in the world.

Roberts said he could set up a demonstration machine with that much memory, so Paul flew to Albuquerque with his precious cargo of code written on punched paper tape. En route, he realized that he had not yet written one part of the program, called the loader. He got out pencil and paper and wrote the code before he reached New Mexico.

2+2=4

Paul had expected MITS to be a large organization with an impressive-looking CEO. Instead, he was met at the airport by a rumpled guy in a beat-up pickup truck; it was Ed Roberts. The MITS office was a grungy storefront in a strip mall.

For his part, Roberts was not impressed with the young kid from Boston, particularly when Paul told Roberts he didn't have enough money for the room that had been reserved for him at the Albuquerque Hilton. Roberts put the bill on his credit card.

The next morning at the MITS office, Paul nervously entered the loader program as Roberts and Yates looked on. He instructed it to run, and for fifteen minutes paper tape streamed through the machine's reader. Finally the teletypewriter attached to the computer clacked out a return message: MEMORY SIZE?

Paul took a deep breath. He typed in the amount of memory, and the computer responded by writing READY. Paul typed in PRINT 2+2, and the teletype answered back: 4.

It worked! Paul and the MITS owners were elated. They immediately began to talk about leasing the rights to the program. Before a deal could be struck, however, Paul returned to Boston and delivered the good news to his partner.

The first step had been taken, and it was triumphant. Now the challenge was to build on it.

Chapter 4

Microsoft Is Born

It was an intense relationship: Gates the workaholic code writer and competitor, Allen the dreamy visionary.
                    —journalist Walter Isaacson

P AUL WAS SOON back in Albuquerque, this time with a job: vice president in charge of software for MITS. Bill remained at Harvard's Aiken Lab.

There was trouble when Bill was discovered breaking several rules: using more than his share of computer time, using the university computer for profit, and using the Defense Department's computer network to store work at another facility.

These serious charges carried the possibility of expulsion. Bill wrote an essay defending himself, however, and in the end suffered nothing worse than a reprimand.

Birth of a Company

During the summer, Bill traveled to Albuquerque and in August a company was born. At first, the firm's name was Micro-Soft, then MicroSoft; within a few months, Bill and Paul had settled on the now-familiar spelling.

Bill wanted the partnership to be structured 60/40 in his own favor, and he persuaded his friend to agree to this arrangement on the grounds that Paul, as an employee of MITS, had fewer financial worries. The initial investment in the firm was $910 for Bill and $606 for Paul.

Microsoft first operated out of a small apartment. Soon, however, it moved to a house, then to offices in a commercial building. The changes were needed because new programmers had arrived. Microsoft's first salaried employee was former Lakesider Marc McDonald. Two other friends, Ric Weiland, whom Bill and Paul had known since the days of the LPG, and Harvardite Monte Davidoff, came on board and were paid by the hour.

That summer MITS shipped the first commercial version of BASIC. Within weeks, users were sending back suggestions for debugging it and using it in new ways, such as games.

However, Bill and Paul were wary of being associated only with MITS. Other companies were developing computers similar to the Altair, and they were interested in Microsoft's product. Furthermore, MITS hardware had a reputation for unreliability. Bill and Paul thought it was only a matter of time before other companies overtook MITS.

The team continued to work on an updated version of BASIC for a new machine that MITS was designing around a new chip manufactured by an Intel rival, the Motorola 6800. At the same time, they worked on versions that would run on competing machines.

Microsoft's first commercial offices were in this building in Albuquerque, New Mexico, from September 1976 to December 1978. The growing company's appetite for more space was brought on by the arrival of programmers needed to improve Altair software and develop new programs for competing machines.

A Stack of Yellow Legal Pads

As autumn approached Bill prepared to return to Harvard. The update for the 6800 Altair, however, was not finished. Bill checked into the Albuquerque Hilton—the hotel Paul had not been able to afford on his first visit—for a final marathon session. He entered with a stack of yellow legal pads and emerged a few days later with a sheaf of scribbled notes in time for a nonstop session at MITS's computer terminal. The program was up and running mere hours before Bill boarded his plane.

Microsoft negotiated the following agreement with MITS for the new version: MITS gave Microsoft a flat fee of $31,200; in return, MITS had the right to bundle copies of the program with its hardware. Bill and Paul shrewdly retained ownership of the program, which they licensed to MITS on a nonexclusive basis.

This meant that Microsoft was free to sell its program, MS-BASIC, to other computer companies, such as Tandy (the corporation that owns Radio Shack) and Commodore.

In these negotiations, Bill took the lead. "I always focused on new ideas and creating new technology," Paul says of those years. "Bill would occasionally jump in and get involved in that, but he was always more focused on the business side."[40]

Your Own Nuclear Sub

In this passage from Wallace and Erickson's *Hard Drive*, MITS executive Ed Curry reflects on the excitement surrounding the early microcomputers.

> You've got to remember that in those days, the idea that you could own a computer, your own computer, was about as wild as the idea today of owning your own nuclear submarine. It was beyond comprehension. Computers were things that were housed in big buildings and took up several floors and had a staff to maintain them and a priesthood to watch over them. A large part of the success of the Altair and the microcomputers that followed was the desire of people just to own one. It didn't really matter if they could do anything with the computer. Everybody knew you could do something with them, but nobody knew what. The mere fact that you owned a computer was very prestigious.

At the same time, Bill was still intensely involved in the nuts-and-bolts work of writing code. He recalls:

> In the first four years of the company, there was no Microsoft program that I wasn't involved in actually writing and designing. In all those initial products, whether it was BASIC, FORTRAN [another computer language], BASIC 6800, or BASIC 6502, not a line of code went out that I didn't look over.[41]

Software Piracy and the Homebrew Computer Club

During the next winter, Bill wrote a public letter that caused a major stir in the small but passionate community of computer enthusiasts. His statement, which appeared in a newsletter for Altair users, defined software as the creative product of hard work. Bill argued, as well, that software should be protected by copyright just like songs or books.

As the computer revolution gathered momentum, the philosophy of copyright and ownership outlined by Bill in 1976 would have important consequences. In the mid-1970s, however, it was a strange and unpopular stance. The general atmosphere was loose, and there was a sense that computers were simply a cool hobby. Most enthusiasts felt that programs were written for fun by people like themselves and should be freely available.

The controversy arose when Steve Dompier, a member of the Homebrew Computer Club, a computer group in the San Francisco Bay area, visited MITS and took home an early version of BASIC. He showed the program to fellow Homebrewers and later published its code in the group's newsletter.

Someone made copies and distributed them at a Homebrew meeting. Despite its many bugs, the program was copied again and distributed widely—and so became the world's first pirated software.

Bill felt that groups like Homebrew were ripping off his hard work. Implying that pirating software was as bad as stealing a computer, he supported his point with sarcasm: "Who cares if the people who worked on [software] get paid?"[42]

Many were outraged by Bill's attitude. Scathing letters in various newsletters denounced him as greedy and uncaring. Undaunted, he continued to defend himself in print.

An Open Letter

In February 1976, Bill Gates wrote "An Open Letter to Hobbyists," which was featured prominently in Altair's *Computer Notes*. The letter summarized Gates's views about ownership of software and the free-wheeling nature of early computing. This excerpt is reprinted in Manes and Andrews's *Gates*.

Almost a year ago, Paul Allen and myself, expecting the hobby market to expand, hired Monte Davidoff and developed Altair BASIC. Though the initial work took only two months, the three of us have spent most of the last year documenting, improving, and adding features to BASIC. . . . The value of the computer time we have used exceeds $40,000.

The feedback we have gotten from the hundreds of people who say they are using BASIC has all been positive. Two surprising things are apparent, however.

1) Most of these "users" never bought BASIC (less than 10 percent of all Altair owners have bought BASIC), and

2) The amount of royalties we have received from sales to hobbyists makes the time spent on Altair BASIC worth less than $2 an hour.

Why is this? As the majority of hobbyists must be aware, most of you steal your software. Hardware must be paid for, but software is something to share. Who cares if the people who worked on it get paid?

Is this fair? One thing you don't do by stealing software is get back at MITS for some problem you may have had. MITS doesn't make money selling software. The royalty paid to us, the manual, the tape and the overhead make it a break-even operation. One thing you do do is prevent good software from being written. Who can afford to do professional work for nothing? What hobbyist can put 3 man-years into programming finding all bugs, documenting his product and distribute for free? . . .

I would appreciate letters from anyone who wants to pay up, or has a suggestion or comment. . . . Nothing would please me more than being able to hire ten programmers and deluge the hobby market with good software.

Beginning Growth

The personal computer market was showing signs of growth. One estimate in the mid-1970s suggested that it was earning $27 million annually. Microsoft, still a tiny company, but already a leader in software, stood to catch a significant chunk of those earnings.

As predicted, other companies had entered the personal computer market. Bill's formula to get their business was simple but effective: make Microsoft's product so attractive that there was no other practical choice.

He did this by offering MS-BASIC at a very low price. Of the early years of the company, Bill writes, "We didn't want to give anyone a reason to look elsewhere. We wanted choosing Microsoft software to be a no-brainer."[43]

Among the companies that negotiated with Microsoft were Commodore, Tandy, and General Electric. Such contracts were big boosts for the little company.

Things were going so well that late in 1976 Paul left MITS and joined Microsoft full-time. Meanwhile, Bill was increasingly dissatisfied at school. The business in Albuquerque appealed to him far more. Early in 1977, Bill dropped out of Harvard.

In the days before floppy disks and CD-ROMs, computer programs were stored on punched paper tapes. A reel similar to this one was used to load Gates and Allen's version of the BASIC program into the Altair 8800 computer, which was then able to perform simple computations faster and more efficiently.

Dropping Out

Bill's family had always stressed academic achievement, and his parents were very upset at his decision to leave the prestigious university. In addition, Mary Gates had just been appointed to the University of Washington's board of regents, the body that oversees policy for the school. How would it look for her to have a dropout son?

The Gateses asked a family friend, a Seattle businessman and philanthropist named Sam Stroum, to try to talk Bill into changing his mind. When Bill was back in Seattle for a visit, Stroum took him to lunch.

Stroum did his best to convince Bill of the importance of staying in school. Instead, Bill gave the older man a compelling vision of a revolution that was going to change the world, referring of course to the intense activity under way and rapidly increasing in the field of computers. In the years since, Stroum has delighted in telling reporters that the one mistake he made in life was not giving Bill Gates a blank check over lunch that day.

As for Harvard, Bill wryly notes that the door is theoretically still open: "I never really made a conscious decision to forego a degree. Technically, I'm just on a really long leave."[44]

Conflicts

In some ways the people who worked at Microsoft and the employees of MITS were compatible. They shared the same hard-core work ethic, a sense of being on an exciting adventure, and a nearly religious zeal about computers.

But there were conflicts, especially the tension between Ed Roberts's low-key style and Bill's in-your-face method of resolving differences. Roberts recalls,

> We got so we didn't even invite him to meetings . . . because he was impossible to deal with. . . . Paul Allen was much more creative than Bill. Bill spent his whole time trying to be argumentative and not trying to come up with solutions. Paul was exactly the opposite.[45]

The distance widened after Roberts sold MITS to a larger company, Pertec. The result was Microsoft's first serious challenge involving business sense rather than technical know-how.

Pertec's lawyers argued that because their client had acquired MITS's assets, the larger firm thus owned the rights to MS-BASIC. Pertec sued to keep Microsoft from licensing its BASIC elsewhere and got a court injunction forbidding Microsoft from granting additional licenses until the matter was resolved.

This put Microsoft in serious financial trouble. Bill's parents offered a loan.

In the fall of 1977, however, a court ruled that Pertec was wrong. Microsoft was free to license to anyone. As Microsoft programmer Steve Wood remarks, Pertec had seriously underestimated its opponent's business capabilities:

> They came in very arrogant, essentially saying, "We are this huge multimillion-dollar company and you are just a handful of kids and we are not going to take you seriously." And that was a big mistake.[46]

Growing

Once Microsoft was free of the injunction against licensing MS-BASIC, several companies that had been waiting hurried to acquire the right to use the company's software. By late fall of 1977, all the main contenders in the low end of the microcomputer market ran versions of Microsoft BASIC. Microsoft's end-of-year income figures reflected this growth spurt. The company took in almost $400,000. Bill and Paul's share came to a little over $37,000 split between them.

As business grew, so did the company. In addition to several new programmers, Microsoft gained its first secretary, a woman in her forties named Miriam Lubow.

Miriam knew nothing about computers, but she fit in and became an informal den mother for the Microsofties, as they called themselves. In particular, she was a kind of personal assistant to Bill. She made sure he ate properly, slept enough, changed his clothes occasionally, and got to the airport for business trips with more than a few minutes to spare.

Someone who would play a large role in Microsoft's future was also hired during this period. This was Vern Raburn, who had first been an enemy.

A few years before, Raburn had formed a small company to develop a version of BASIC for a now-forgotten microcomputer. When his coders tried to pirate Microsoft's version, Bill threatened legal action.

Raburn dropped his plans and instead became a pioneer in retail software, which until then had been mostly sold by mail order. As Microsoft became more interested in marketing, Bill persuaded his onetime foe to join the company.

No one at Microsoft had managed a company. Tried-and-true methods for running a successful firm were virtually unknown to the officers and other top staffers. Instead, an atmosphere of constant near-chaos prevailed.

There was no full-time receptionist, so phone calls were answered and visitors met by whoever was available. Work was periodically interrupted by competitions, such as battles to see who could write code in the fewest bytes. The Microsoft way of holding a meeting was to see who could yell the loudest.

The general hiring technique was to find smart, driven people, give them a job, and expect them to do it with minimal guidance. Bill would challenge a new recruit with a taunt like, "I could write this in BASIC over the weekend." The unspoken message was: You'd better be able to do it, too. Journalists Stephen Manes and Paul Andrews write,

> The self-motivated, hardcore programmers Gates hired would take the bait again and again. Somehow, partly through personal charisma, partly through the power of the dare, Gates got his legions to stick with him through all the noise.[47]

No Life

Bill's characteristic pattern during the Albuquerque years—hard work and more hard work—still typifies Bill and Microsoft. By all accounts, Bill had virtually no personal life during this period, though he did find time to take occasional breaks.

For instance, he retained his fondness for movies. A fan of sports cars, he also fulfilled a longtime dream by buying a Porsche 911, the first in a succession of expensive, fast cars.

Bill loved to race the flashy 911 along the steep mountain roads outside Albuquerque. Despite his penchant for detail, however, Bill was oddly careless about maintaining his car. He once burned out the 911's engine by ignoring the low-oil light.

He was equally negligent about obeying the written rules of the road. His glove compartment was reportedly stuffed with parking tickets, and his love of fast driving made him well known to the police.

Part of Bill's legend from this period, in fact, is that he lost his driver's license for speeding and that this event quickened Microsoft's move from New Mexico. The story appears to be untrue.

It is true, however, that Bill was thinking about relocating. Following the conflict with Pertec, there was nothing to keep Microsoft in New Mexico. And there were plenty of reasons to leave. For example, Microsoft was having difficulty luring employees to the small, isolated desert town. Also, Bill and Paul, along with several other Microsofties, were Pacific Northwest natives. They missed the cool, mild climate, the abundant water, and their families.

Leaving New Mexico

Microsoft's young leaders first considered a move to northern California. Paul, however, argued in favor of the Seattle area. He pointed out that in northern California, already home to many computer-related firms, top-notch employees would be subject to tempting offers of other jobs.

Paul also argued that California's high living expenses meant correspondingly high salaries. In Seattle, on the other hand, Microsoft could offer the benefits of living in the Pacific Northwest and at the same time get away with paying lower wages.

In early 1978, a decision was reached. By the end of the year, the company would relocate to Bellevue, a suburb just across Lake Washington from Seattle. It was the end of one era and the beginning of another.

Chapter 5

Return to the Northwest

The revenue from that partnership [between IBM and Microsoft] gave Gates a guaranteed income stream and the push he needed to make his vision—Microsoft software on every desktop PC—come true.

—journalists James Wallace and Jim Erickson

TWELVE OF MICROSOFT'S thirteen employees made the move to the Northwest late in 1978. The exception was Miriam Lubow.

Microsoft's new offices were on the eighth floor of a modest office building in Bellevue. Bill's parents threw a welcome party, and then it was back to work.

Attention

Although still a relatively small company, Microsoft was growing fast. In the year following the move, its workforce more than doubled. By the end of 1981, it would have more employees than Bill's father's law firm.

There was also a change in direction. Vern Raburn had been trying to convince Bill that the future lay in retail, selling software for ordinary secretaries, businesspeople, and others who used computers but were not expert programmers.

Bill, however, had been indifferent about the needs of these so-called end users. He thought of them only as people who wasted his time with dumb questions. He was more comfortable dealing with programmers, who understood his language.

What convinced Bill to change his mind was the success of VisiCalc, the first widely popular spreadsheet program. When Bill saw that VisiCalc was earning a fortune for VisiCorp, a rival company, he decided that similar products might be good for Microsoft. Following through, he created a consumer products division, with Raburn its head. Its first releases were a typing tutor and a game, a modest beginning for a group that would eventually account for nearly half the company's revenues.

As it grew, Microsoft began receiving attention from companies interested in buying it out. One was Electronic Data Systems, the Dallas firm headed by billionaire and future presidential candidate Ross Perot.

Accounts vary as to how much Perot offered Bill. Estimates are as far apart as $6 million and $60 million. In any case, the two could not agree and the deal collapsed. With characteristic bluntness, Perot later expressed regret: "I should have just said, 'Now Bill, you set the price, and I'll take it.'"[48]

Bill reviews paperwork in his Bellevue, Washington, office. In 1978 Microsoft moved from Albuquerque to this Seattle suburb to attract new employees and ease the homesickness of its company's founders.

Ballmer's Back

Bill knew that Microsoft's management and business structure needed streamlining. There were no middle managers, for instance; most employees reported directly to Bill. Since his time was taken up with day-to-day problems, Bill had little time to concentrate on broader issues. Ignoring Paul Allen's contribution, Bill recalls:

> When we got up to 30 [employees], it was still just me, a secretary, and 28 programmers. I wrote all the checks, answered the mail, took the phone calls—it was a great R&D [research and development] group, nothing more.[49]

In addition, many of the company's business practices were surprisingly outdated. For example, Microsoft used handwritten ledgers for bookkeeping purposes. Clearly, the company needed help to make the transition from a small, informally run firm into one with a solid managerial foundation.

For this, Bill enlisted his old Harvard friend Steve Ballmer. Interested in marketing, Ballmer had worked at Procter & Gamble and had attended Stanford Graduate School of Business. Early in 1980, Bill hired him as Microsoft's assistant to the president.

The new business chief soon proved he could match Bill in the shouting matches that characterized Microsoft's executive style. "Our first major row came when I insisted it was time to hire 17 more people," Steve recalls. "He claimed I was trying to bankrupt him."[50]

"Part of Who I Was"

Ballmer prevailed, and for the first time experienced managers oversaw financial, legal, and personnel aspects of the company.

Ballmer's boisterous, over-the-top style offended many Microsofties. They were further alienated by his generous salary and benefits; employees who had given their all to the company for years weren't even getting overtime pay. Also, Ballmer's efforts to formalize operations did not sit well with the independent-minded, laid-back programmers. Several resigned in disgust.

Due to rapid expansion in 1980, Gates hired Steve Ballmer (pictured) to streamline Microsoft's management structure and modernize its business practices.

But the business chief's arrival was a crucial turning point; he eventually played a major role in Microsoft's future success. Bill remarks:

> I always knew I would have close business associates like Ballmer . . . and that we would stick together and grow together no matter what happened. I didn't know that because of some analysis. I just decided early on that was part of who I was.[51]

By 1980, the personal computer business was taking off. Revenues were doubling annually, with predictions of a billion dollars for 1981.

Tandy, Apple, and Commodore were still leading, although other manufacturers were entering the market. Among these were Hewlett-Packard, Wang, Xerox, and the biggest of them all, IBM.

Big Blue, as IBM was nicknamed after its trademark color, had dominated the mainframe computer market for many years. Now, having long ignored personal computers, it was finally working on one.

As plans for the new machine were being formulated, IBM made a critical decision. Certain pieces of hardware and software, it was agreed, would come from existing technology that IBM would buy or lease from other companies.

This decision spared IBM from the time-consuming process of developing equipment and programs from scratch. It also gave the resulting computer an open, or "clonable," architecture; that is, the entire unit was easy to copy. The success of the IBM PC and "IBM-compatible" clones would in time make IBM the industry standard.

Among other things, IBM needed programming languages. For these, the choice of vendor was clear: an enterprising firm in Bellevue, Washington. IBM contacted Microsoft and set up a meeting for July 1980. It was a small move in a project that was not the most important one on Big Blue's schedule. But it was an event that would have a dramatic impact. Bill remarks:

> The power of the machine . . . the endorsement by IBM of using a personal computer, and then the critical mass of software, distribution, and peripherals that came along with that [made] it the biggest milestone in the history of personal computing. It was a sea change.[52]

Big Blue Meets the Microsofties

The contrast between the formal, suit- and wingtip-wearing IBM engineers and the casual Microsofties could not have been greater. "Ballmer figures he was invited," writes journalist Paul Carroll, "because his one year at business school meant that he was the only one at [Microsoft] who knew how to wear a suit."[53]

Still, Jack Sams, the engineer leading the IBM group, was surprised at how large and pleasant the Microsoft offices were. He had been expecting more modest surroundings.

Sams was also impressed with the energy, brains, and openness of the company's leader. Bill had good reason to be on his best behavior; a job for IBM would be far and away his biggest project yet. Sams recalls:

> I knew Bill was young, but I had never seen him before. When someone came out to take us back to his office, I thought [he] was the office boy. It was Bill. . . .

> I told IBM executives [later] that by the time you were with Bill for fifteen minutes, you no longer thought about how old he was or what he looked like. He had the most brilliant mind that I had ever dealt with.[54]

The meeting went well. Microsoft agreed to supply four languages, including BASIC, for IBM's top-secret new machine.

Digital Research Drops In

IBM still needed another important piece of software: an operating system. How it found one has become one of the best-known stories in the computer industry.

Operating systems are the base that other software runs "on top" of; they do much of the unseen but crucial work. Journalist Fred Moody explains: "An operating system is a computer's consciousness—the software that turns a set of chips, wires, boards, and other components into a functioning brain."[55]

As of 1980, several competing codes were vying to become the standard operating system for microcomputers. Virtually every manufacturer had a different system, and none was compatible with the others. It was a confused and crowded field.

One system was considered superior by most programmers: Control Program for Microcomputers, or CP/M. CP/M had been developed by a Pacific Grove, California, company called Digital Research (DR).

DR was headed by Gary Kildall, an old friend of Paul's and Bill's. Kildall had been a graduate student at the University of Washington when the younger men had been at Lakeside, and they had often hung out together.

When the IBM engineers mentioned that they were looking for an operating system, Bill suggested that they contact his friend Gary. Bill even set up a meeting between Kildall and the IBM engineers for the following day.

Digital Research Drops Out

There are several versions of what happened next. There is agreement, however, that when the IBM engineers arrived in Pacific Grove for their appointment, Kildall was not there. He was out flying in his airplane, apparently headed to another business meeting.

It is not clear why Kildall chose not to meet with Sams and his colleagues. Some observers say he simply was not much interested in the IBM contract, that he thought it would not be very important.

In any event, the IBM engineers were greeted by Dorothy McEwen, Kildall's wife and the company's vice president. Before any discussion began, however, the engineers wanted McEwen to sign a nondisclosure agreement, which would prohibit her from repeating the contents of their conversation elsewhere.

McEwen refused. She thought the proposed agreement was one-sided in IBM's favor, and she was wary of the big company's intentions. Eventually a compromise was reached, but the relationship between the two firms was never smooth and, in the end, IBM chose not to deal with Kildall.

As relations between IBM and Kildall broke down, Bill and Paul made a bold offer. They told IBM they could supply an operating system.

It was an enormous undertaking, especially considering IBM's tight deadlines. But Bill and Paul decided they wanted a bigger piece of the project. Bill notes, "IBM . . . had a real chance to create a new, broad standard in personal computing. We wanted to be a part of it."[56]

Big Blue Goes with Microsoft

Bill and Paul had an advantage. They knew that a Seattle programmer, Tim Paterson, had already developed an operating system similar to CP/M that would meet IBM's specifications with only some modification. Paterson's program was called 86-DOS (short for 8086 disk operating system) or Q-Dos (short for quick and dirty operating system).

Bill and Paul were sure they could license DOS from Paterson and his employer, Seattle Computer Products. They were also certain they could hire Paterson, on a contract basis, to modify the program.

IBM agreed to the proposal and drew up a contract with Microsoft.

Gary Kildall's loss to Bill Gates points up one of the key factors in Bill's character: his ability to take an idea and make it commercial. Computer journalist Stewart Alsop writes:

> Kildall is very smart. He can spot an important technology before anybody else. . . .
>
> But Gates has something extra. . . . Gates can see not only the important technology but how to get that technology into the marketplace in a big way. And he's willing to do whatever is necessary to make that happen.[57]

Tim Paterson, the Seattle programmer who played a crucial role in fulfilling Microsoft's bold promise to supply IBM with an operating system for its new personal computer. Known as MS-DOS (disk operating system), this software went on to earn billions of dollars for Microsoft.

Nonexclusive

The exact numbers have never been made public, but it is estimated that IBM paid Microsoft about $500,000 as an advance
against royalties, for the four languages plus the operating system, which became known as MS-DOS.

The contract was nonexclusive—that is, Microsoft was free to
license its work to other parties. Bill and Paul had learned from their
problems with Pertec to make nonexclusivity a vital condition.

In retrospect, IBM should have tried to modify or eliminate
the nonexclusivity condition. Big Blue assumed, incorrectly,
that the money was in their product, hardware, not in software,
which was Microsoft's base. This error cost IBM billions of dollars that went instead to Microsoft. Journalist John Seabrook
notes that software's "lack of physical existence" makes its
importance easy to underestimate:

> I.B.M., which was one of the great business organiza-
> tions in history, and which was perfectly placed to own
> the personal-computer business, disastrously failed to
> appreciate the importance of the software Gates
> designed for it.[58]

Bill, however, did grasp it. He remarks:

> Our restricting IBM's ability to compete with us in
> licensing MS-DOS to other computer makers was the
> key point. . . . We knew that good IBM products are usu-
> ally cloned, so it didn't take a rocket scientist to figure
> out that eventually we could license DOS to others.[59]

The PC was indeed cloned cheaply by other manufacturers.
But the same was not true for Microsoft's products. No one
knew how to clone MS-DOS, and so Microsoft collected a fee
every time a PC or a PC clone was sold.

Hard-Core Again

The companies signed the contract in November 1980. For the
occasion, Steve wore a suit; Bill wore a sweatshirt.

Bill, Paul, and the rest of the company went into hard-core
mode. Fourteen-hour days were the norm. Everyone survived

on hamburgers from the Burgermaster across the street and unlimited free Cokes, which had become a Microsoft tradition.

The schedules were brutal. All of Microsoft's work was due in stages in just over a year. As if the deadlines weren't bad enough, IBM seemed to do everything possible to slow things further. For example, IBM engineers kept making changes in the hardware, and each change meant multiple software changes. Every afternoon, someone would round up the disks with Microsoft's latest modifications and get them to the airport in time for the overnight delivery service to IBM's project offices in Boca Raton, Florida.

Tim Paterson had been hired as an outside contractor. Several Microsoft programmers were assigned to help him. However, under IBM's security rules, Paterson could not know the client's identity. For months, he labored in seclusion for this mystery client.

In May 1981, Paterson left Seattle Computer in a dispute with the company's owner. He immediately began work for Microsoft as a regular employee, and finally got to see Microsoft's prototype of the machine he had been working on.

Hal in Chains

Microsoft's prototype of the IBM machine was nicknamed Hal, after HAL, the single-minded computer in the film *2001: A Space Odyssey.*

There was a problem with Hal: It was supposed to be top secret, but Microsofties were accustomed to bringing anyone by to see it—girlfriends, pals, other computer enthusiasts. They also were casual about leaving the prototype out in the open during working hours.

IBM was worried about the smaller company's lax sense of security. Eventually, IBM insisted that Hal stay in a windowless closet at the end of a hall. The closet was supposed to be locked all the time, even when people were inside, working on the computer. But in this sweatbox atmosphere the closet got so hot that the machine began to malfunction. Days of precious work time were lost to heat-created glitches.

In the end, the Microsoft programmers kept the door open as they worked, closing it quickly if an IBM representative was spotted. It was usually Steve Ballmer who went crashing around the office, yelling that Big Blue was on the way. Paul Carroll writes that people would then "rush to hide all the documents and hardware that were supposed to be under lock and key."[60]

Finally, an Announcement

By the spring, word was out in the computer community that IBM was planning something big.

Meanwhile, Bill and Paul had tried to buy 86-DOS from Seattle Computer instead of leasing it. Their initial offer of $30,000 was met by a counterproposal: $150,000.

Bill yelled and said that the figure would bankrupt him. In the end they reached a compromise: Microsoft bought the system outright for $75,000. Considering the fortune Microsoft later gained, it was the deal of the century. At the time, however, the future success of MS-DOS, the adapted program, was by no means certain.

Bill Gates (right) and Paul Allen stand next to Microsoft's prototype of the IBM PC one month before "Big Blue" announced its debut in July 1981. Nicknamed "Hal"— after the computer in 2001: A Space Odyssey—the prototype was often left out in the open in Microsoft's offices despite IBM's strict requirement for secrecy.

"Oh, Come On"

When asked what kind of person he hires for Microsoft, Bill's standard response is that he chooses smart people. Asked "How do you define smart?" by *Playboy*'s David Rensin in an interview published in July 1994, Bill rolled his eyes impatiently and replied:

> Oh, come on. It's an elusive concept. There's a certain sharpness, an ability to absorb new facts. To walk into a situation, have something explained to you and immediately say, "Well, what about this?" To ask an insightful question. To absorb it in real time. A capacity to remember. To relate to domains [areas] that may not seem connected at first. A certain creativity that allows people to be effective.

Tim Paterson was a Microsoft employee, but he was still a shareholder and director of Seattle Computer. As such, he had a stake in selling 86-DOS for a reasonable price. He reviewed the contract before it was signed and thought it fair:

> We had no idea IBM was going to sell many of these computers. They were a stranger to this business. Somehow, people seem to think we had an inkling it was going to be this big success. I certainly didn't. So buying DOS . . . was a massive gamble on Microsoft's part, a 50/50 chance.[61]

On August 12, 1981, IBM officially announced the arrival of the IBM PC.

Chapter 6

Computer Wars

I'm very involved in my work, and I take it seriously. If something goes by me of inferior quality, I don't say, "Hey, let's go get a beer," or, "Hey, how about a vacation?"

—Bill Gates

FOR IBM IN 1981, the PC was not a major project. Calling it "a little foray by a small group" within Big Blue, Bill says that "IBM was more interested in proving it could do something quick than exactly what happened with the product."[62]

To everyone's surprise, millions of people bought the machines. The PC's phenomenal success helped to usher in the computer age and spurred the fierce competition that characterized the latter part of the decade.

Revolution

Paul Carroll notes that in the 1980s the PC helped IBM "produce the greatest profits any company has ever turned in."[63] Microsoft's role in the phenomenon, however, was not guaranteed.

IBM was still exploring alternative operating systems, any one of which could have replaced DOS. Worried, Bill tried to cement DOS's position by making it the cheapest system for IBM to license.

Meanwhile, as he had predicted, most computer manufacturers followed IBM's lead. Companies like Compaq and Digital began cloning IBM's hardware—and clones needed the same operating system.

Bill quickly struck deals with these manufacturers. In this way, although many experts found CP/M superior, DOS became the dominant system for personal computers. Fred Moody writes, "The sheer numbers of manufacturers and early high-volume sales . . . made the DOS-based design the immediate world standard."[64]

The exception was Apple Computer. The Cupertino, California, firm retained a completely different design for both its hardware and operating system, eventually emerging as the only major personal computer maker that did not use DOS. The rivalry between IBM and Apple, which sharply divided champions of their different operating systems, is still going on.

Some critics argue that this contest severely limited freedom of choice. However, it also simplified a confusing field. Bill comments:

> Now we have just the two architectures. . . . Back in the good old days we had 30 or 40 different machines that were totally incompatible. . . . Because we've brought millions and millions of people in, we've had to make it more homogeneous, more standardized.[65]

Two children use an IBM PCjr to learn how to read and write. Less expensive—and less capable—than the PC, this machine failed to thrive in the booming market established by its "senior."

(Left to right) Steve Jobs meets with Apple president John Sculley and cofounder Steve Wozniak at the unveiling of the Apple IIc in April 1984. Using hardware and operating software much different than those of IBM and Microsoft, Apple introduced the "mouse" and graphical user interfaces (GUIs) that made personal computers much easier to operate.

GUIs

Apple was headed by another boy wonder: the charismatic Steve Jobs, whose vision was to make a machine that was affordable, reliable, and easy to use.

This last idea was an important selling point; many people were intimidated by the complex DOS commands. Jobs believed that the answer was an operating system called a graphical user interface, or GUI, which had been experimentally developed by Xerox at its Palo Alto Research Center, Xerox PARC.

Unlike DOS, GUIs did not respond to typed-in commands alone. They also used a pointer, called a mouse, and pictures called icons. Today these features are commonplace, but at the time they were radically different. Unfortunately, Apple's first machine using a GUI was a flop. At $10,000 the Lisa was too expensive for the average user, and so slow that it inspired a joke:

"Knock knock."
"Who's there?"
(15-second pause) "Lisa."

When the Lisa failed, Jobs concentrated on another machine, the Macintosh. For much of its applications software, Jobs turned to his friend Bill Gates, whom he had known for years, in the spring of 1981 when Microsoft was laboring to finish DOS for IBM.

Bill was still cool to the idea of spending time and resources on developing applications. However, DOS and the PC were not yet successes. Bill reasoned that working with Apple on a rival system would be a prudent bet. He agreed to develop several programs for the Mac.

Expansion

Meanwhile, Bill also dealt with expansion in his own company.

At the end of 1979, Microsoft had 28 employees and sales of about $2.4 million. Two years later, it had sales of $16 million, 130 employees, and over $1 million in the bank. By the end of another year it would double to 200 employees and sales of $32 million.

All this required space. The company took over the top floor of another building. In addition, expansion on this scale required a president, someone to oversee areas like manufacturing and

A Big Table

The casual approach to security at Microsoft changed drastically once the partnerships with IBM and Apple began. *Hard Drive* authors Wallace and Erickson quote Microsoft programmer Bob Wood.

Before the serious work started with IBM, everything was out in the open, on tables. . . . Everything that was going to happen in the personal computer world was [there]. There was no real secrecy and nobody thought much about that. But then IBM imposed a lot of secrecy. And that was true of the Macintosh work. It got to the point where you knew there was going to be an industry announcement about a new computer. . . .

Some of the offices were covered with computer paper on the inside, so you couldn't look in them, and you knew there was a private project in there. Then you would read in the newspaper that a new computer had been announced, and you would walk down the corridor and all the paper had come down on one of the offices, and there was the new machine.

finance. This would free Steve to concentrate on marketing and Bill to focus on product development. Microsoft's first choice was not a good fit and lasted less than a year. He was replaced with Jon Shirley, a Tandy executive with a reputation as a tough negotiator.

Shirley was also an effective buffer between Microsoft employees and the abrasive personalities of its executives. Former Microsoft employee Raymond Biley said the new president was easy to work with: "He helped round out the team. He wasn't like Bill or Steve Ballmer. He had kid gloves. He was more able to make you feel good about a bad decision and re-direct your efforts."[66]

Paul Departs

Soon after Shirley's arrival, illness created another dramatic change.

In the fall of 1982, while in Europe, Paul Allen fell ill. Back in Seattle, he was diagnosed with lymphoma, a form of cancer. Fortunately, it was a treatable kind called Hodgkin's lymphoma. Paul underwent two courses of radiation therapy and recovered.

The incident, however, shook Paul deeply. He realized how many things he wanted to do in life but had put off in favor of work. By the spring he had resigned and was on an extended trip to Europe.

Bill was, by all accounts, devastated. He wanted and needed Paul nearby, and was miserable without him. Paul was the visionary, the one who could see deeply into the future while Bill concentrated on the hard business details.

Some observers have suggested that Bill didn't fully understand the seriousness of Paul's illness. Others speculate that he may have understood it well. An early episode of colitis, such as Bill suffered as a teenager, can be a strong indicator of future colon cancer.

"Running for President"

Microsoft had been slowly developing its own GUI since 1981, ever since Steve Jobs had shown Bill the still-secret Macintosh. In the fall of 1982, however, Bill made GUIs a top priority.

Paul Allen left Microsoft in 1983 after learning that he had Hodgkin's disease. Fortunately the condition was treatable, but Paul's departure had a devastating effect on Bill, who had long relied on his friend's visionary talents.

The stimulus came from VisiOn, a flashy new product from a rival company. VisiOn used a mouse and a graphical interface to run integrated software—programs that worked together so that a user could easily switch from performing tasks on, say, a word processor to working on a spreadsheet or database and back again.

The bad news for Bill was that VisiCorp had publicly displayed a wonderful product. The good news was that VisiOn, like the Mac, was still under development, which gave him time.

Bill assembled a team to work on something he called Interface Manager, soon renamed Windows. The team was told to deliver their baby to the world by April 1984.

By early 1983, a demo was ready. It showed overlapping windows, apparently running simultaneous programs. In fact, none of them did anything; it was an illusion.

Bill used the first Windows demo to drive the same strategy that had worked with BASIC for the Altair: promise a product, get the contract, then write the code. He relentlessly lobbied computer manufacturers and software developers to commit themselves to using it. He also relentlessly hyped Windows to the press and the general public.

Las Vegas was the scene of an all-out blitz when the city hosted Comdex, the computer industry's major annual trade show. Taxis had Windows ads. Rental-car agencies handed out Windows keychains. Every hotel room had a Windows plastic bag slipped under its door. The hoopla caused computer journalist Esther Dyson to comment wryly, "Microsoft is running for president."[67]

Vaporware

As it turned out, the VisiOn threat faded. Its parent company was having financial and legal troubles. Both company and product became casualties in the fast-moving computer wars.

Nonetheless, Windows was a huge gamble for Bill's small consumer applications division. Journalist Statford P. Sherman wrote in 1984 that if Windows succeeded, a new generation of programs would be needed for DOS users—programs Microsoft was preparing to supply: "If it fails to become an industry standard, [however,] Microsoft may not get another chance to take the consumer market by storm."[68]

As the release date approached, problems kept cropping up. Windows slipped behind schedule, and the deadline was pushed back several times.

The development team grew increasingly frustrated. Several top people left, victims of burnout, during the long and painful period of Windows's birth. Many on the team called the final grueling months of work "the death march."

As the Windows release date was pushed further into the future, the press began to ridicule its nonarrival. They called the program "vaporware," a promised product that never appears. Bill was known as the Viscount of Vapor.

Finally Released

In the fall of 1985, over a year and a half after its first promised release date, Windows 1.0 finally shipped.

At its launch, Microsoft was at last able to turn the tables on those who had made fun of the new product. At one event, the Windows Roast, Bill was awarded the Golden Vaporware Award. He and Steve also sang a duet of "The Impossible Dream."

Despite all the work and publicity, however, the final product was unimpressive. It still had hundreds of bugs. Users also complained about its overall slowness and the shortage of applications that would run on it.

Many people, including some Microsoft executives and industry insiders, felt that the project had been an enormous mistake. Bill's persistence eventually paid off, however, when over time Windows triumphed. "We bet the company on Windows and we deserve to benefit," Bill observes. "It was a risk that's paid off immensely. In retrospect, committing to the graphics interface seems so obvious that now it's hard to keep a straight face." [69]

Look and Feel

Just before Windows's release, a major problem arose. At issue was something that Steve Jobs had worried about for a long time: the strong resemblance between Windows and the Mac, which had been released in 1984.

Microsoft programmers working on software for the Mac had used the Mac operating system for years when it was under development. Apple's attorneys argued that these programmers

An Apple Macintosh computer. Microsoft's first version of Windows had a similar screen format, so much so that Apple took legal action. Gates exercised his shrewd business skills to avoid a damaging lawsuit and gain Apple's permission to retain portions of the Mac technology for use in Windows.

had stolen many of the Mac's best features, including the command bar, the control panel, the trash can, and the menu concept. The Mac's so-called look and feel—the user's basic perception of a machine—had, the attorneys said, been stolen.

When Apple filed a complaint, threatening to take Microsoft to court in 1985, Bill's response was immediate and harsh. Impossible, he said; his programmers had been careful to use only visual displays that Microsoft had created or otherwise had a right to use.

But Bill was eager to avoid a lawsuit. A public battle just before the Windows release would have been disastrous, so the companies worked out a compromise. Microsoft gave Apple certain business concessions and changed Windows to make it less obviously Mac-like. In return, Microsoft got a nonexclusive license to use portions of the Mac technology for Windows.

This was seen by many as a victory for Microsoft. Bill had made only minor concessions, received a valuable license, and avoided a harmful lawsuit.

The two software executives still sparred, however. When Steve Jobs complained that Microsoft had stolen Apple's ideas, Bill mocked this by pointing out that much of the basic work had been done years before, not at Microsoft or Apple but at Xerox's PARC:

> I think it's more like we both have this rich neighbor named Xerox, and you broke in to steal the TV set, and you found out I'd been there first and you said, "Hey, that's no fair! I wanted to steal the TV set!"[70]

New House

Bill's focus for years had been on business. He was so focused that he had disconnected his car radio, and he refused to own a TV because it would have been distracting. He remarked in 1984, "I still come home every night to my IBM-PC. I don't play the violin, you know."[71] However, Bill did sometimes take breaks. He and his friends would go to the movies or play games like Trivial Pursuit.

In this period British-born Estelle Mathers took over as Bill's personal assistant. She was responsible for calling and

Cats and Dogs

In this excerpt from *I Sing the Body Electronic*, journalist Fred Moody describes the sharp contrast between Mac and IBM users.

> The two types were as opposite and nearly incompatible as cat people and dog people. Mac people were free thinkers with artistic temperaments, given to reacting emotionally to issues and only occasionally following up with more or less rational arguments. DOS people, in their own view, were purely analytical thinkers whose approach to computing problems was scientific, rational, and unclouded by emotion. Each claimed to see profound shortcomings and failings in the other, and the two groups disagreed on virtually everything.

waking her boss in time for meetings. She drove him to the airport, reminded him to comb his hair, and told him what to wear. Bill was constantly losing his credit cards and traveler's checks, so he also relied on her for ready cash.

One significant event in his private affairs during the 1980s was the purchase of a house. He had always rented, but in 1983 he bought a forty-four-hundred square-foot waterfront home, half a mile from the house he'd grown up in and where his parents still lived.

He asked his mother and grandmother to decorate it, and they had furniture moved while he was on a trip to Japan. On his return, the jet-lagged executive had to call Estelle Mathers and ask which house to go to.

Girlfriend

Bill had dated various women over the years, but it was not until the spring of 1984 that he seriously began going out with someone.

Ann Winblad was an entrepreneur from Minneapolis. She had founded a software firm for $500, sold it for several million dollars, and relocated to the Bay Area. According to one story, the quick-witted Winblad was the originator of the word "vaporware."

In some ways Bill and Ann were quite different. She was a vegetarian, for instance. For a time she succeeded in exchanging the junk food in Bill's usual diet for healthier alternatives, though he has since gone back to eating meat.

In other ways they were well matched. They shared a love of movies, and sometimes, when they were in different cities, went on what they called virtual movie dates. That is, they would attend the same movie at more or less the same time, discussing it on their car phones on the way to and from the theaters.

More importantly, Ann was Bill's intellectual equal. They would take "theme vacations" together, bringing along stacks of books about particular subjects such as bioengineering, physics, and human evolution.

Emotionally, Ann was also Bill's match. She would stand up to his more outrageous behavior with an equal intensity. Journalist Walter Isaacson notes, "They were kindred minds as well as spirits."[72]

The Public Image

As his company's fortunes became more prominent in the public eye, so did Bill.

He had been a well-known figure within the computer industry since the beginning of his career, but Bill was barely known outside it. During the 1980s, this changed dramatically.

Pam Edstrom, Microsoft's public relations manager, began fostering her boss's "boy genius" image in the media. In 1983 Bill was named one of *People* magazine's "25 most intriguing people."

In early 1984 a major article and full-page photo appeared in *Fortune*, a leading business magazine. In April Bill was on the cover of *Time*, and at the end of the year *Esquire* chose him as one of the "best of the new generation." By 1985, he was on *Good Housekeeping*'s list of the fifty most eligible bachelors, along with Warren Beatty, Michael Jackson, and Burt Reynolds.

As might be expected, exaggerated claims sometimes overshadowed the truth. The company was hailed in the popular press for creating "slick, tight code" even as experts complained about Microsoft's slow and bug-filled products. Bill's stint at TRW occurred in ninth grade, according to one press release, not the twelfth, and Microsoft's early earnings were inflated.

Despite the inconsistencies, the public relations blitz worked. Within a few years, Bill was a celebrity. Journalists Steve Manes and Paul Andrews wryly comment, "As a

Gates in 1984. With his oversized glasses and unruly hair, Bill became the "boy genius" of Microsoft when the public took notice of his company's rapid success in the mid-1980s.

spokesman for himself and Microsoft, Bill Gates did just fine, especially if you didn't bother to check the facts."[73]

Spectacular Benefits

The computer revolution continued to gain momentum. In 1982 *Time* had proclaimed the personal computer "Man of the Year." By 1984, when the Mac was released, the revolution was in full swing. Hardware manufacturers shipped 5 million machines in America that year, and the foreign market was nearly as large. The software industry was also booming. People everywhere were discovering how spectacularly useful and fun personal computers could be.

Microsoft was reaping the benefits. In 1984 it was the second fastest growing company in Washington State. For the fiscal year ending July 1984, it had sales of $100 million, making it the first microcomputer software company in the world to reach that magic number. It was also bulging at the seams, with seven hundred employees spilling out into additional rented space. That summer, Jon Shirley sent out a memo: within a year the company would be moving to permanent offices.

As 1985 drew to a close, Microsoft's prospects might have been summed up by one of the computer world's favorite phrases: "insanely great." At parties celebrating, among other things, Bill's thirtieth birthday, spirits were high. Microsofties presented him with a mock cover of *Time*, with BILL in place of the magazine logo and a prominent headline: "Microsoft Releases Gates 30.0." At a costume party, Bill came as Jay Gatsby, the glittering and wealthy character from Fitzgerald's novel *The Great Gatsby*.

Things were moving fast, Bill was a celebrity, and the company had grown far beyond even his expectations. But there was much more to come.

Chapter 7

New Location, New Power

> *Gates has clearly won. The revolution is over, and the free-wheeling innovation in the software industry has ground to a halt. For me it's the Kingdom of the Dead.*
> —former Lotus chairman Mitch Kapor

FOR ITS PERMANENT location, Microsoft bought four hundred acres of land in nearby Redmond and built four buildings. A fifth was already under construction when the move took place early in 1986.

New Campus

The new site mixed Microsoft informality with subtle designs to improve productivity. For example, almost everyone had a private office in the modern two-story structures, often with an outside view.

In good weather, people ate outside or took juggling breaks. In bad weather, games like bowling were played in the hallways. Many new employees, fresh out of university, must have felt as though they were still at college.

Randall Stross notes that the complex was even called the Microsoft campus. "Microsoft wanted an environment," he writes, "that would resemble the college campuses from which many of its software developers had been directly lifted."[74]

A Mix

Relaxation was important, but some aspects of the buildings' design nudged employees toward maximum productivity.

Most of the offices were the same size, though Bill's and Jon Shirley's were slightly larger. This made moving easy. Since the company was constantly being "reorged"—reorganized into new groups—workers changed offices about every six months.

The campus was not close to retail shops or restaurants, so employees were less tempted to spend time eating off-site or shopping. On the other hand, it was close to highways to Seattle and the surrounding suburbs, and thus commute time was minimal.

On-site cafeterias offered a variety of good food at low prices. This was another incentive not to leave the campus. Seating in the cafeterias was limited, however, so employees often took food back to their offices and worked while they ate.

Finally, parking slots were unreserved. This policy rewarded early birds with a spot close to the building— a definite advantage in the Northwest's rainy weather.

Microsoft's current headquarters, or "campus," in Redmond, Washington. Its collegelike environment promotes both productivity and relaxation.

Going Public

Soon after the move, the company went public. That is, it offered for sale shares of itself, which could be bought by the general public and traded on a stock exchange.

According to several sources, Bill was never comfortable with this public offering. Although going public was going to make him extremely rich, it also meant he would have less control over his business. When a company is privately held, it is not obliged to release much information about itself, and the executives have flexibility in running the firm's affairs.

A company that goes public, however, must answer to stockholders. Bill didn't much like the idea of being responsible to other people.

However, the public offering had to happen. For one thing, many Microsoft employees owned stock, which was virtually useless to them unless it could be publicly traded. Since Microsoft offered few other benefits to its hardworking employees, going public was one way to keep them from jumping ship by finding jobs elsewhere.

In any event, a company that has five hundred employees who are also stockholders is required by law to go public. That time was coming soon for Microsoft.

A Rich Man Now

Bill had a reputation for being tight with money. He had always refused to fly first class, for instance. Even for the grueling schedule required for the promotion of the initial public offering of Microsoft stock—eight cities around the world in ten days—he wanted to fly coach.

However, the company underwriting the sale, Goldman Sachs, convinced Bill to go first class. The investment brokers told him that *he* was the product being sold—his confidence, energy, and brains were what convinced investors to buy. He needed to be alert and fresh, they said, and so he agreed.

En route to Europe, Bill calculated the difference in price between coach and first class: about $200 for every hour of flight time. Each hour, he woke up the representatives from Goldman

Gates in his office in Redmond. Although most offices are roughly the same size on the Microsoft campus, Bill's is slightly larger and has a view of the surrounding buildings and landscape.

Sachs who were traveling with him. He then asked them for $200, demanding to know whether first class was worth the money.

This apparently obsessive worry about money may have been offset somewhat by the showing Microsoft made on its first day of sale in March 1986. The opening price was $25.75 per share, a relatively high figure for a first offer. By the end of the day, on which 2.5 million shares were sold, the price had climbed to an even more impressive $27.75.

Bill sold shares worth about $1.7 million and kept enough to own 45 percent of the firm. By the end of the day, he was worth about $311 million. Paul Allen, Jon Shirley, Steve Ballmer, and two other Microsoft executives, Charles Simonyi and Gordon Letwin, also became multimillionaires that day.

Lose a Battle, Gain a Visionary

In the summer of 1986, someone came on board who would fill an extremely important role at Microsoft. Nathan Myhrvold, a former student of the great physicist Stephen Hawking, is universally credited with having an intellectual bandwidth equal to that of

Bill Gates. Myhrvold's serious interests besides technology include paleontology and French cooking. "I don't know anyone I would say is smarter than Nathan," Bill says admiringly. "He stands out even in the Microsoft environment."[75]

Myhrvold now occupies Paul Allen's old seat as Microsoft's resident visionary, a person who sees deeply into the possibilities of the future. Randall Stross writes, "Myhrvold, who had no formal training in computer science or engineering, [is now] piloting Microsoft's technical direction."[76]

Myhrvold soon headed up an elite unit dedicated to studying extremely advanced technologies. Bill saw this R&D work as essential to staying ahead of the competition.

Problems with IBM

Microsoft and IBM had never been comfortable with each other's methods.

One reason was that Microsoft liked to use small, efficient teams, whereas IBM routinely assigned huge numbers of engineers to a given project.

IBM liked to measure its progress by the amount of code written; Microsoft prided itself on writing as little code as possible, an approach that often requires far more work. Also, for IBM the most important goal was meeting deadlines. Microsoft changed product requirements as it went along and kept release dates flexible.

A serious conflict arose when IBM decided to stop the clone market by making its latest PC, the 286, impossible to copy. This was a potential disaster for Microsoft.

Windows was not part of IBM's new plan. Instead, IBM was developing Hawthorne—an entirely new GUI, incompatible with Windows. It seemed that all the time, work, and money Bill had put into Windows for IBM might be wasted.

Bill met with IBM executives to convince them to incorporate Windows into Hawthorne. He was able to get a tentative commitment from IBM: a short period to study whether Microsoft could work with the Hawthorne team.

Two weeks of daily meetings followed. In the end, Microsoft prevailed. IBM agreed to work with Microsoft on a new project called Presentation Manager (PM) that combined the systems.

The youth and energy of the smaller company had prevailed over Big Blue's size. Referring to the six Microsofties who had squared off against IBM's thirty engineers, Myhrvold dryly comments, "We knew we had them outnumbered."[77]

The Compaq Alliance

IBM released the 286 in April 1987. It looked like another disaster for Microsoft.

For the moment, the 286 ran on good old MS-DOS, but the plan was to eventually switch to a new, IBM-controlled operating system. This would mean the end of royalties for Microsoft.

Bill reacted by forging an alliance with Compaq, a Texas-based computer manufacturer. He committed to creating a version of Windows for Compaq's new Deskpro 386. The Deskpro was based on a faster and more powerful chip than the 286's, which Bill had long ridiculed as "brain-dead."

The alliance was a direct challenge to IBM. Before, Big Blue had always set the standard. Now Compaq and Microsoft were throwing down a challenge: the most powerful personal computer in the world. Compaq's president confidently told reporters that the Deskpro would be the new standard.

Compaq did not take over, but it did make a significant dent in IBM's dominance of PCs. In 1987 Compaq's market share rose significantly while IBM's dropped. Bill comments:

> That was the first time people started to get a sense that it wasn't just IBM setting the standards, that this industry had a life of its own, and that companies like Compaq and [chip maker] Intel were in there doing new things that people should pay attention to.[78]

Billionaire Baron

Microsoft stock hit new highs, and the *Wall Street Journal* of March 20, 1987, announced that Bill Gates had become a billionaire; not only that, but he was the youngest billionaire in history, not counting those who inherited their wealth. That same year the company saw $345.9 million in revenues, listed more than eighteen hundred employees, and became the number-one PC software company in the world.

Around this time, there was a gradual change in the public perception of Microsoft and its leader. Bill-bashing, as it was dubbed, began in the computer industry press and spread to the general press and then to the public. It was a kind of backlash to the public relations drive that had made Bill so famous a few years earlier.

In part, this negative feeling focused on sheer size and wealth. But Bill was no longer seen as a benign, boyish genius for other reasons, as well.

As stories circulated of his relentless quest to win at any cost, people both inside and outside the industry increasingly regarded him as a power-hungry tycoon. Newspapers compared him to the so-called robber barons, who made great fortunes in land and railways in the late nineteenth century.

Now Microsoft was increasingly seen as a monster that swallowed everything in its path. The company was even accused of sabotaging new technology that threatened its dominance. The

Bill and a colleague review design options for future Microsoft products and upgrades. As the company grew in size and wealth, the public image of Gates changed from that of "boy genius" to "robber baron." The U.S. government would soon share this view.

term "getting micro-slimed" was used to describe the fate of a company that had been crushed under the power of the software giant. Computer journalist Stewart Alsop characterized the general attitude at the time:

> It's remarkable how widespread the negative feelings toward Microsoft are. You now have not only software applications but hardware companies worried to one degree or another about Microsoft's control of the business. That's unheralded.[79]

Microgames

As might be expected, throughout the 1980s most of Bill's energies were devoted to running his increasingly powerful company. He did take some time off for recreation, however.

One break involved the building of a summer retreat called Gateaway. Gateaway was in part a tribute to Gam, Bill's grandmother, who died in 1987. The retreat was on Gam's beloved Hood Canal, where Bill had spent his childhood summers. It had a tennis court, spa, and four woodsy houses—one for each of the Gates kids, plus a bigger one for Bill Senior and Mary that also doubled as a corporate retreat.

The Microgames, a fancy version of the Cheerio Olympics from Bill's childhood, became a yearly tradition at Gateaway. Selected employees and their families engaged in a series of

Giving the Other Dogs a Chance

In his article "E-Mail from Bill," published in the *New Yorker* in 1994, John Seabrook quotes Scott McNealy, the head of Sun Microsystems, on the ferocity of his longtime rival.

> I like Bill. Bill is a smart guy. But I think the problem is that Microsoft has caught the bunny. You know, when you go to the dog track they have that mechanical bunny that makes the dogs run? Well, sometimes a dog is so fast he catches the bunny and then the other dogs don't run anymore. That's the situation in the software business today: Bill has caught the bunny. I admire Bill for catching the bunny, but now we can't have a race. He ought to be loosed from the bunny, to give the other dogs a chance.

tests, such as puzzle-solving, singing, racing, water sports, and treasure hunts. Bill's father recalls, "There were always a couple of mental games as well as performances and regular games."[80]

The Microgames became increasingly elaborate. For one sandcastle-building contest, Bill had six tons of sand brought in. For a Wild West theme, the closing event was a smoke-signal contest, which the contestants called "low-tech data communication." Entertainment was provided by country singer Kris Kristofferson.

Bill, as usual, was relentless in his quest to win. One year the theme was "African Safari." He and his girlfriend of the time had prepared by spending part of a vacation memorizing all the countries of Africa and their capitals, because he knew one of the contests would involve filling in a map of Africa within two minutes. The couple won.

Windows Wins

The 1990 edition of Windows, release 3.0, hit the market in the spring of that year.

Microsoft spent millions advertising it, kicking the campaign off with a huge New York show that reportedly cost $3 million. The campaign worked, and the heavily hyped program became the best-selling software product in history.

After the initial wave of interest, however, bugs began to show up. There were problems installing Windows on certain machines, problems with networks, problems with mouse operation, and even data-destroying crashes. It seemed that Microsoft was guilty, as in the past, of shipping a product too quickly.

In the end, though, the problems hardly mattered. By Christmas, sales were pushing 2 million. The price of Microsoft's stock headed straight up, and it became the first software company to do a billion dollars in annual revenue. Windows was finally justifying Bill's stubborn backing.

A Divorce?

Meanwhile, the old "look and feel" charge from Apple came back to haunt Bill.

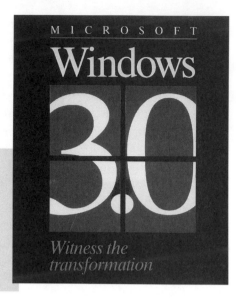

A poster advertising Windows 3.0. Released with much fanfare in the spring of 1990, this version firmly established Microsoft's position as the premier supplier of computer software, despite initial problems with the product.

Apple acknowledged that it had granted Microsoft a license to use Macintosh-like features for Windows 1.0. However, a new lawsuit charged that those features were not covered for newer versions of Windows. Microsoft, Apple charged, was in violation of its contract. It was the beginning of a court case that would drag on for years.

At about the same time, relations between IBM and Microsoft were growing worse by the day, as deadlines for various projects closed in. Teams worked nonstop and shuttled frantically between development sites, but each project had serious problems. Communication deteriorated, and in mid-1990 the companies agreed that they could no longer work together.

In the press, the incident was widely reported as "a divorce." Bill writes in his book *The Road Ahead,*

> We worked extremely hard to make sure our . . . work with IBM succeeded. I felt [it] would be a ticket to the future for both companies. Instead, it eventually created an enormous rift between us.[81]

End of the Decade

Microsoft's year-end party for 1990, rumored to have cost $1 million, typified the glitzy, fast-track decade that had preceded it.

Eight thousand guests and employees took over the enormous convention center in downtown Seattle. In true Pacific Northwest style, some party-goers wore formal evening wear while others came in parkas and jeans.

The theme was "Holiday in Manhattan," complete with actors portraying panhandlers and cops. There were replica delicatessens, museums, nightclubs, even a Coney Island–style amusement park for kids.

Newspapers complained about the irony of actors playing panhandlers while genuinely homeless people froze outside; Microsoft spokesmen responded by pointing out that all the left-over food was donated to charity.

Bill, dressed in a red tuxedo, was in a relaxed and friendly mood. The next morning, however, a Sunday, he was back at work. There was plenty to do.

Chapter 8

Balancing Family and Work

Microsoft has been the single greatest beneficiary of inept competition of any company in the world.
—former Microsoft executive Vern Raburn

FOR BILL GATES, the 1990s have been dominated by several major events. He and his colleagues encountered several business challenges, including a major probe by the U.S. government and the unexpectedly strong showing of the Internet. On a personal level, Bill continued to build a massive showcase house on Lake Washington; he also married and became a father.

FTC Probe

For much of the decade, Microsoft has been enmeshed in a complex legal investigation, as the federal government studies claims that Microsoft's very strong position among the software companies strangles competition. Unfair domination over an industry by a single firm is called monopoly and is against U.S. law. The Federal Trade Commission (FTC) is responsible for forcing monopolistic companies to divide, giving others room to compete.

The FTC probe identified several areas of concern. One was Microsoft's practice of offering discounts on MS-DOS for every computer shipped with the company's operating system. The FTC worried that computer manufacturers had little incentive to consider other systems that might have cost less or served end users better.

Another concern was the incomplete separation between Microsoft's systems division and its applications division. Using antitrust legislation developed during the time of the railroad barons, the federal investigators tried to show that a complete separation between these groups was necessary.

The invisible division was sometimes called a Chinese wall, and sometimes likened to the separation in government between church and state. The idea was that Microsoft applications teams should not be allowed to have previews of changes in upcoming operating systems.

According to the government, and to the many industry spokesmen who were critical of Microsoft, such insider knowledge gave Microsoft's application teams an unfair advantage over outside, independent developers. Microsoft was therefore guilty of monopolistic practices, by not holding its own applications division back.

After visiting a Washington soup kitchen, Bill is greeted by fans and reporters. During the 1990s, Gates and Microsoft would come under extreme public and government scrutiny.

"A Job-Creating Machine"

In a letter to the editor published in the August 16, 1993, issue of *InfoWorld,* Bill Gates responds to charges that Microsoft is unfairly monopolistic and powerful:

> The entire software industry is showing healthy growth. Far from suffocating the industry, Microsoft, through its systems products, has stimulated the creation not just of new jobs but the founding of hundreds of whole new companies as well. Far from stagnating, the software and hardware industries are alive with innovation. And customers benefit from a market that creates intense competition through high-quality products at low prices. . . . In total, more than 16,000 software companies spread throughout the United States . . . are now involved in development for Windows. . . . Windows is nothing less than a job-creating machine.

At first, Microsoft executives insisted that such a division did exist within the company. Gradually they acknowledged that there was, in fact, some swapping of information between the two divisions. Eventually, Microsoft took the offensive, arguing that the idea of separation was a foolish and outdated notion, and that what the company was doing was simply smart business. It made no sense, they argued, to deliberately hold themselves back. Nonetheless, critics came back with the charge that, even if Microsoft was not doing something illegal, it was certainly testing the limits of ethical behaviors.

Sabotage?

Deep discounts and possible inside knowledge raised serious questions of conduct that was improper but not necessarily illegal. What troubled the FTC most was allegations that Microsoft was sabotaging competitors.

For instance, a rumor had spread widely that DR DOS, made by rival Dell Computer, would not work with Windows. In fact, it would.

The trouble arose with a "beta" or test version of Windows distributed to tens of thousands of experienced computer users, who were expected to identify bugs and suggest improvements. Some beta testers found that when they tried to use DR DOS on a Windows-equipped computer, an error message popped up, directing the user to call Microsoft for assistance. Critics asserted that Microsoft had deliberately programmed Windows to reject the rival operating system to scare customers away from DR DOS. This was a serious charge, since beta testers tend to be knowledgeable people whose collective opinions carry considerable weight in the broader user community.

Taking the allegations together, the FTC decided that Microsoft's business practices bordered on the unethical. Many agreed. Gary Reback, a lawyer who represents several Microsoft competitors, states, "[Microsoft is] trying to use an existing monopoly to retard introduction of new technology. . . . They have a game plan to monopolize every market they touch."[82]

Bill insisted that his actions were simply smart business. He told reporters, "In the future, maybe our competitors will decide to become more competent."[83]

Justice

Bill refused to make changes in the way he did business. Frustrated after four years of investigation that had failed to result in anything concrete, the FTC handed the investigation over to the U.S. Department of Justice in 1994.

The new investigation was hampered in two main ways. Evidence against Microsoft was conflicting and weak, and, perhaps more crucially, there were seemingly compelling reasons to go easy on Microsoft. For example, it was mainly thanks to Microsoft that the United States was the world leader in software. As America was outpaced by other countries in other areas of manufacturing, many leaders looked to software as a means for the country to retain its competitive edge. Darker reasons were rumored, as well, such as the report that Bill and Steve had indicated to Vice President Al Gore that they would take Microsoft out of the country if the government moved to force a breakup.

In the summer of 1995, the probe was called off. In exchange, Microsoft agreed to make minor changes in its business arrangements.

Microsoft's competitors were outraged, feeling that the government had not been thorough enough in its investigation. Recently, moreover, Microsoft has been accused of violating the terms of the Justice Department agreement. Asked by a reporter why his competitors still complain, Bill replied: "Well, we're very successful. But I think it's very draining to fool yourself into thinking that you'll be able to hobble Microsoft. That's not right. It's not gonna happen."[84]

Mr. Gates Builds His Dream House

Throughout the 1990s, Bill has increasingly turned his attention to nonbusiness matters.

He has never lavished great amounts of money on himself, though there are exceptions. Far and away the biggest personal expenditure so far is the bold new house he is building for himself.

As far back as 1984, Bill was telling reporters about the kind of home he wanted to build someday. His idea was to create a showcase exploring the outer limits of high-tech housing.

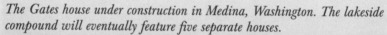

The Gates house under construction in Medina, Washington. The lakeside compound will eventually feature five separate houses.

In 1988 he bought land in Medina, an upscale neighborhood on Lake Washington near the Microsoft campus. After getting rid of the million-dollar house that came with the property (it was barged to a new location), Bill conducted an international competition for an architect.

The winning entry was an understated, low-key design resulting from a joint venture between a Pennsylvania firm and a Seattle architect. The Gates compound comprises five timbered houses, a twenty-car underground garage, a separate house for a caretaker, and other outbuildings. From the lake, however, one sees only the five timbered houses, none higher than two stories. Terraced into the hillside, the houses appear unattached, though they are connected underground.

One of the main houses is essentially a grand entry hall. Another has guest bedrooms, a fourteen thousand book library, a small movie theater, and a dining room. The third has a large reception hall; the fourth is a beach house with dock, a sixty-foot pool, and a hot tub. At the top, isolated from the rest, is Bill's private home.

Scattered throughout are amenities such as an exercise room, computer centers, and a game room. Altogether, there will be forty thousand square feet of living space—roughly twenty times more than the average American home.

High-Tech House

The cost of the waterfront complex, originally estimated at $15 million, has skyrocketed to at least $40 million. Still under construction after nearly a decade, it is a popular tourist attraction for boatloads of people who sail past it every day.

The architects have made the house as environmentally sensitive as possible. Much of the timber is recycled from an old lumber mill, for instance, and about one-third of the property is slated as wetlands.

But the house will also be a showcase of high-tech wizardry. Over a hundred microprocessors will control its electronic and mechanical functions. For instance, visitors will receive pins encoded with their preferences in visual art, music, and movies.

The Gates compound nears completion in September 1997. Incorporating both the old and the cutting-edge—recycled timbers and the latest sensors and microprocessors—Bill envisions his house as a showcase for future home technology.

A person's favorite images will be displayed on monitors built into the walls. When that person moves to a different room, the art will "follow."

In *The Road Ahead*, Bill remarks on the experimental nature of his house:

> I enjoy experimenting, and I know some of my con-
> cepts . . . will work out better than others. Maybe I'll decide
> to conceal the monitors behind conventional wall art or
> throw the electronic pins into the trash. Or maybe I'll grow
> accustomed to the systems in the house, or even fond of
> them, and wonder how I got along without them.[85]

Some critics say that Bill is unrealistic to call his home a model for the future. David Enna, home editor of the *Charlotte Observer*, notes that except for insulation, construction techniques for houses have changed little in the last forty years. He doubts that the average home owner will rush to embrace Bill's vision:

Although builders have been promoting "Smart House" technology for years, it has been very slow to catch on. . . . I believe Americans will furiously resist jamming technology into their homes.[86]

First Comes Love . . .

The 1990s have also seen serious changes in Bill's romantic life. Though they have remained close friends, Bill and Ann Winblad broke off their relationship in 1987. The next year he met Melinda French, a Microsoft product manager nine years younger than himself. Melinda grew up in Dallas, where her father was an aerospace engineer. She attended Duke University, where she received bachelor's degrees in computer science and engineering and a master's in business administration—all within five years. She then went to work at Microsoft.

Like Bill, she was focused and ambitious. But she was also more at ease socially and more health-conscious. She regularly worked out and ate a diet more balanced than Bill's habitual hamburger fare.

Friends agreed that overall the couple was well matched. "Melinda is a very good companion for Bill," according to Vern Raburn. "She's funny, very engaging in conversation, intelligent, and super-intense."[87]

. . . Then Comes Marriage

Bill and Melinda had a long-running on-again, off-again relationship and at one point broke up for nearly a year before reuniting.

By mid-1992, however, the relationship had grown more serious, and Mary Gates was chiding her son for taking so long to settle down. Indeed, she soon began inquiring pointedly when Bill was going to ask Melinda to marry him. At the time, few outsiders knew that Mary had been diagnosed with breast cancer; the romance may have been helped along by Mary's desire to see her son wed before she became extremely ill.

When Bill finally popped the question and Melinda accepted in March 1993, he secretly diverted a northwest-bound jet the

Bill and his wife, Melinda, attend a Seattle SuperSonics basketball game. They met in 1988 while she was working as a product manager at Microsoft and were married after several years of on-again, off-again courtship.

couple had chartered, making a surprise stop in Omaha, Nebraska, the home of Bill's friend Warren Buffett. The billionaire investor had arranged for a jewelry store he owned to be open on a Sunday morning so that Melinda could pick out a ring.

An unpleasant aspect of Bill's fame cropped up when the engagement was made public: Tight security was required around Melinda. There had already been some frightening incidents involving the Gates family's safety. In 1984 someone had tried unsuccessfully to kidnap Mary, and on another occasion someone had pulled a knife on Bill.

A less serious note was sounded by the spate of jokes on talk shows and elsewhere—measures of how Bill's wealth had elevated him to a status usually reserved for movie stars. People like *Tonight Show* host Jay Leno mused on questions like: What would appropriate wedding gifts be—gold-plated pocket protectors? Not a Nintendo game, but how about Nintendo itself? Or a Waterford crystal computer?

The Wedding

The wedding took place on New Year's Day, 1994, on the Hawaiian island of Lanai.

Security was tight. The flow of people on and off the island, which is almost entirely private, was closely monitored. A phony date was given to the press, and reporters were banned under threat of arrest. Everyone hired to work on the event had to sign a nondisclosure statement.

After the 130 guests had made their way to Honolulu, they were picked up by a chartered jet. They occupied almost all the rooms in the island's two hotels for a week in advance of the wedding itself.

That week saw a number of festivities, and on New Year's Eve the guests were treated to fireworks. Willie Nelson, Melinda's favorite musician, made a surprise appearance that night. One of Nelson's best-received numbers was the old tune "If You've Got the Money, Honey (I've Got the Time)."

The next day, Bill and Melinda were married at sunset on the grounds of the Manele Bay Hotel golf course. Since Melinda is a Roman Catholic, the Reverend William Sullivan, who headed the Jesuit-run Seattle University, officiated. Steve Ballmer was the best man.

Afterward

Mary Gates was at the ceremony, but a few days later she was admitted to a hospital in Seattle. She died in June, at the age of sixty-four. Not long afterward, the Seattle City Council named the avenue leading into the senior Gateses' neighborhood for her, in honor of her many years of service to United Way, the University of Washington, and other institutions. In the years since, Bill Senior has retired and remarried.

Melinda left Microsoft after the wedding, in line with company policy that an employee's spouse should not be his or her boss. She now serves on the boards of Duke University and a philanthropic foundation she and Bill founded.

On April 26, 1996, Melinda gave birth to Jennifer Katharine Gates. For reasons of security, Melinda had entered the hospital

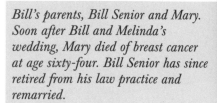

Bill's parents, Bill Senior and Mary. Soon after Bill and Melinda's wedding, Mary died of breast cancer at age sixty-four. Bill Senior has since retired from his law practice and remarried.

under an assumed name, and the birth was kept secret for three days. By then, Melinda was home and Bill was back at work.

For someone who had shown little interest in children and was given to declarations such as "Kids are a subset," Bill seemed to respond positively to fatherhood. He carried a photo of Jennifer in his wallet and joked that now there was something besides his competitors keeping him up at night.

In the spring of 1997, the Gates family moved into their still-unfinished home.

In some ways Bill appeared to be mellowing as he reached middle age. On the other hand, being a husband and a father has not seemed to slow down his business instincts. Speaking of his competitors, he says, "If they really think I'm going to work a lot less just because I'm married, that's an error."[88]

The Net Nearly Slips By

Bill nearly did miss out on a technological development that may become as momentous as any major aspect of the computer revolution.

The importance of the Internet is clear today, even as it morphs constantly and companies vie for Net-based advantages. But in the early days, no one predicted the dramatic capacity of the Net to connect people and supply information. Bill admits his own failure to pick up on what he has since described as "the most important single development in the world of computing since the IBM PC was introduced in 1981."[89]

The Internet evolved from a small electronic network begun in 1969 as a means of sharing research among four major contractors for the U.S. Department of Defense. At first it was the domain of academics and the military, though it opened up somewhat to the public with the development of software that allowed the use of graphics and linkage to other documents.

A computer enthusiast explores the World Wide Web at a "cyber-café." Together, the Internet and the Web are the next quantum leap in computer applications and commerce, a field in which Microsoft and rival Netscape are struggling for dominance.

Still, Internet use was limited, mainly through commercial online services such as America Online (AOL) and CompuServe. Not until the development of the software called Web browsers did the Net really take off. Web browsers allow easy access to the World Wide Web, the gateway to cyberspace that runs on top of the Internet. When a Web browser was offered free in 1993, millions of people downloaded it for their own use.

No Rules

In the early 1990s the World Wide Web was a freewheeling collective that resembled in spirit nothing so much as the early days of computer hackers.

There were no rules in this new territory, and new possibilities opened up every day. The big online service providers scrambled to supply browser technology for their subscribers, while students in computer labs all over the world applied fresh ideas to the challenge.

By the fall of 1993, an estimated 15 million people were surfing the Net. Commercial sites on the Web had gone from about fifty to about ten thousand in six months. The volume of traffic was doubling every four months.

Not Paying Attention

Bill Gates, however, was not paying attention. There are several reasons for this uncharacteristic failure to anticipate a major trend in the use of computers. One stemmed from a security measure Microsoft executives had approved—the virtual sealing off of the company from the Internet. Rather, Microsoft had its own communications system, an "intranet" of thirty thousand in-house computers. With sensitive e-mail making the rounds daily, the company's executives wanted to prevent industry rivals from accessing trade secrets.

Thus, use of the Net was essentially banned in all Microsoft offices. The only way to gain access on campus was to sign in and out of the computers in the main library. Some Microsoft employees were surfing the Net on their computers at home, but still, as of 1994, most college kids knew more about the Net than Microsoft's people did.

Playing Catch-Up

Another reason for Microsoft's late entry into the competition for the online dollar was that the company was confidently—or arrogantly—pursuing a different path.

Bill had authorized development of a browser, Internet Explorer, in the summer of 1994. He was more interested, however, in ventures like Microsoft Network (MSN), the company's online service.

Bill was fascinated by the intersection of Microsoft with cable and entertainment companies. In interviews, he began talking about his version of the information superhighway: television receivers as powerful tools for interactive TV and information on demand.

A small California company, Netscape, had in the fall of 1994 posted a free test version of the most sophisticated net browser any Internet surfer had ever seen. Netscape's executives gave away their browser free for a reason. They were hoping that

Gates announces Microsoft's Internet strategy in July 1995. Bill has devoted a large part of his company's energies and resources into developing and marketing a Web browser—Internet Explorer—to compete with Netscape's Navigator.

increased browser use would create a demand for Web server software, which is essential for companies wanting to do business on the Web, and which Netscape could sell at a profit.

The strategy worked, and Netscape's fortunes soared. When it went public, the firm zoomed to a value of over $3 billion.

Bill's non-Net ventures, meanwhile, were slow in development and poor performers in the marketplace; one industry analyst called MSN the Yugo of online services. Belatedly, Bill realized that the Internet was the wave of the future. It looked like Netscape was setting the standard in cyberspace—and end running Microsoft, just as Microsoft had once bested IBM.

No one is certain what the next step will be. However, in the opinion of business journalist Randall Stross, the unexpected challenge was a shot in the arm for Bill:

> [B]y all the evidence, he positively relished the jolt out of complacency that Netscape had given his company. . . . He was correct in his assessment that challenges brought out the best in the company.[90]

The future for Bill will undoubtedly involve balancing such business challenges with the responsibilities and challenges of family life.

Into the Future

Every so often he gets one of these visions—and boy, is he tena-cious.
—former Microsoft executive Tom Corddry on his boss

THE BILL GATES story is still evolving, and new developments take place daily.

Microsoft's chief continues, of course, to be immensely wealthy, though he does his best to downplay this aspect of his success. Bill's standard response to questions about money is that he owns Microsoft stock, not dollars: "So it's only through multiplication that you convert what I own into some scary number."[91]

Nonetheless, Microsoft's spectacular success has put Bill on top of the heap. As of July 1997, his personal fortune was some $36.4 billion. That year he not only headed *Forbes* magazine's annual list of the top business billionaires for the third straight time, but for the first time was slightly ahead of the man who had long been the world's richest individual, the sultan of Brunei.

Still Dominant

As the struggle to control the Internet and other aspects of the electronic age heats up, Bill remains the most important single person in the computer industry.

This position requires a constant shifting of partnerships. For example, in mid-1997 Microsoft announced it was again allying itself with Apple Computer by buying $150 million worth of Apple stock.

Bill's role in keeping the ailing Mac manufacturer alive is partly altruistic. Although if Apple were to fail, Microsoft would

A casual smile and a calm demeanor hide Gates's relentless desire to remain the foremost driving force in software development and marketing. Bill hopes that by diversifying into areas such as Web-based television, film production, and voice-recognition technology, Microsoft will continue to make breakthroughs as it did with DOS.

have a 100 percent share of the PC operating systems market, the Redmond giant would then be vulnerable to additional accusations of industry dominance via monopoly. According to analyst Richard Scocozza, "It's in [Microsoft's] best interest to keep Apple from failing so they don't incur any additional scrutiny from the Justice Department."[92]

Such associations as the Apple/Microsoft alliance can and do shift and change easily. Journalist David Rensin notes, "Given the fluidity of partnerships and strategic alliances in the computer industry, today's friends could easily become tomorrow's foes—and vice versa—if Gates thinks it advantageous."[93]

Still Driven

Critics complain that Bill's take-no-prisoners approach to competition has killed the easy-going atmosphere that characterized the early days of personal computing. Rob Glaser, a former Microsoft executive who now runs a company that makes Internet software, admires his former boss's vision. But, he adds, Bill is relentless:

He doesn't look for win-win situations with others, but for ways to make others lose. Success is defined as flattening the competition, not creating excellence. In Bill's eyes, he's still a kid with a startup who's afraid he'll go out of business if he lets anyone compete.[94]

Others agree that Bill's relentless drive is fueled, at least in part, by fear of losing. "The more successful you get, the higher you climb up the mountain, the farther you have to fall," comments Ann Winblad, with whom he is still close. "I think the fear of the fall gets larger and larger. And I don't think Bill is immune to that fear."[95]

Diversifying

Bill continues to buy or build products he thinks can help Microsoft stay on top.

Some investments have obvious connections that could benefit Microsoft. For instance, Microsoft bought WebTV, a company that sells equipment to let people browse the Web from ordinary television sets. He is also a major investor in SKG Dreamworks, the film production studio founded by Steven Spielberg and others.

Other investments seem to be based more on Bill's personal interests. One of his online ventures is *Slate*, an opinion "magazine" whose content appears on the Internet. *Slate* is edited by Michael Kinsley, former editor of the prestigious *New Republic.*

Bill also invested $5 million in ICOS, a bioengineering company that investigates anti-inflammatory drug therapies for a variety of diseases. Bill is, of course, interested in seeing a return on his money; but he cites personal development as his real reason for investing in ICOS. Specifically, he now has the chance "once a month to get together with two or three really smart biologists and learn about biotechnology."[96]

Within Microsoft, Bill is funding Nathan Myhrvold's advanced research-and-development teams. These groups are working on a number of high-risk projects, such as voice recognition, with no set completion dates or even guarantees of success. Bill remarks:

If you go over to the lab, you'll meet some guys over there who think, "Hey, in two years—no problem." Now because it's their job, they're allowed to be optimistic. But in our business plans, you won't find that dependency written in. And we're willing to fund that work for however long it takes.[97]

Philanthropy

Bill has remarked often that he will continue working as long as he is still having fun. He says: "I think my job is more interesting now than ever, because of the incredible impact that PCs are having [via the Internet]. . . . It's very exciting."[98]

He has also stated that he will retire from running Microsoft within a decade and devote himself with the same intensity to philanthropy—that is, the making of gifts that benefit the community at large, such as donations to charities and arts organizations.

In fact, he promises to give most of his fortune away. He says he plans to leave Jennifer and other children he may have

Incredible Adventures

Bill Gates reflects on his past and future in the introduction to his book *The Road Ahead*.

The past twenty years have been an incredible adventure for me. It started on a day when, as a college sophomore, I stood in Harvard Square with my friend Paul Allen and pored over the description of a kit computer in *Popular Electronics* magazine. As we read excitedly about the first truly personal computer, Paul and I didn't know exactly how it would be used, but we were sure it would change us and the world of computing. We were right. The personal-computer revolution happened and it has affected millions of lives. It has led us to places we had barely imagined.

We are all beginning another great journey. We aren't sure where this one will lead us either, but again I am certain this revolution will touch even more lives and take us all farther. The major changes coming will be in the way people communicate with each other. The benefits and problems arising from this upcoming communications revolution will be much greater than those brought about by the PC.

about $10 million each, because he fears that larger inherited fortunes are "corrupting" and "crippling."

Both Microsoft and Bill were criticized in the past because Microsoft had not made as many major philanthropic contributions as certain other large companies. A longtime friend and supporter of Bill's comments: "He never really grew up in terms of social responsibility and relationships with other people. He's brilliant but still childlike. He can be a fun companion, but he can lack human empathy."[99]

One exception to this poor record is United Way, Mary Gates's favorite cause. Bill and his company have generously supported United Way since the early days of his success.

Recently, the overall picture has improved. Microsoft has created an entire generation of millionaires in the Seattle area; estimates range from two thousand to ten thousand. Many of them, such as Paul Allen, Scott Oki, and Ida Cole, are active in philanthropy.

For his own part, Bill has given $34 million to the University of Washington. Part of this supports research by the distinguished biogenetics scientist Leroy Hood. Bill and Steve Ballmer together donated $25 million for a new computer center at Harvard.

Bill has also given $6 million to Stanford, and he and Paul Allen donated funds for a science center at their alma mater, Lakeside. It is called the Allen/Gates Science Center, because Bill lost the coin toss.

The Gates Library Foundation

Bill's largest single act of philanthropy to date is the creation of the Gates Library Foundation.

A partnership with U.S. and Canadian public libraries, the foundation is designed to bring computers and digital information to communities, with an emphasis on low-income areas that might not otherwise have access to such tools as the Internet. Bill remarks,

> Until we're educating every kid in a fantastic way, until every inner city is cleaned up, there is no shortage of things to do. And as society gets richer, we can choose

to allocate the resources in a way that gives people the incentive to go out and do those unfinished jobs.[100]

Bill and Melinda have pledged $200 million for the project, with software worth another $200 million promised from Microsoft. The money will go for training, hardware, and software for thousands of libraries.

Some observers have pointed out that this philanthropy in fact will benefit Microsoft in the long run, since those who receive free software will have to buy any upgrades from Microsoft. Nonetheless, the foundation's mission statement reflects a commitment to furthering the idea of lifelong learning for everyone.

In addition to catching up in cyberspace, Bill has also made progress in the world of philanthropy. As founder of the Gates Library Foundation, he has pledged millions of dollars to provide both U.S. and Canadian public libraries with access to the information superhighway.

Changing Classrooms

In *The Road Ahead*, Gates discusses the role of computers in education, an issue he is addressing with his philanthropic Gates Library Foundation.

> Some fear that technology will dehumanize formal education. But anyone who has seen kids working together around a computer the way my friends and I first did in 1968, or watched exchanges between students in classrooms separated by oceans, knows that technology can humanize the educational environment. The same technologic forces that will make learning so necessary will also make it practical and enjoyable. Corporations are reinventing themselves around the flexible opportunities afforded by information technology; classrooms will have to change as well.

Looking to the Future

Even though Nathan Myhrvold appears to be the one person at Microsoft most responsible for looking to the future, most of the public still thinks of Bill Gates as the visionary.

In an interview in the spring of 1997, Bill was asked to name the technologies that he thinks "will have the biggest impact on the industry in the next 15 years." He replied:

> Speech recognition, natural-language understanding, automatic learning, flat-screen displays, optic fiber, the continuation of Moore's Law [which states that computers will double in power and speed about every eighteen months]. Those are the key ones.[101]

Of course, no one, not even Bill Gates, knows exactly what form computing will take in the next decade. Former Microsoft executive Tom Corddry remarks, "Everybody in Hollywood, everybody in the book business, in the computer business, is sort of circling one another nervously right now, trying to figure this thing out."[102]

Whatever form "this thing" does take in the coming years, it will no doubt incorporate significant input from Bill Gates.

Notes

Introduction: A Life Less Ordinary

1. John Seabrook, "E-Mail from Bill," *New Yorker,* January 10, 1994.
2. Bill Gates, *The Road Ahead.* New York: Viking, 1995, p. 9.
3. Gates, *The Road Ahead,* p. 15.
4. Quoted in Fred Moody, *I Sing the Body Electronic: A Year with Microsoft on the Multimedia Frontier.* New York: Viking, 1995, p. 82.
5. Quoted in Seabrook, "E-Mail from Bill."
6. Quoted in Randall E. Stross, *The Microsoft Way: The Real Story of How the Company Outsmarts Its Competition.* Reading, MA: Addison-Wesley, 1996, p. 47.
7. Quoted in Stephen Manes and Paul Andrews, *Gates: How Microsoft's Mogul Reinvented an Industry—and Made Himself the Richest Man in America.* New York: Doubleday, 1993, p. 286.
8. Moody, *I Sing the Body Electronic,* p. 81.
9. Quoted in Seabrook, "E-Mail from Bill."
10. Quoted in Walter Isaacson, "In Search of the Real Bill Gates," *Time,* January 13, 1997.

Chapter 1: Childhood

11. Quoted in Seabrook, "E-Mail from Bill."
12. Quoted in Isaacson, "In Search of the Real Bill Gates."
13. Quoted in Manes and Andrews, *Gates,* p. 18.
14. Quoted in James Wallace and Jim Erickson, *Hard Drive: Bill Gates and the Making of the Microsoft Empire.* New York: Wiley, 1992, p. 12.

15. Quoted in Wallace and Erickson, *Hard Drive*, p. 7.
16. Quoted in Manes and Andrews, *Gates*, p. 21.
17. Quoted in Isaacson, "In Search of the Real Bill Gates."
18. Quoted in David Rensin, "Playboy Interview: Bill Gates," *Playboy*, July 1994.
19. Quoted in Isaacson, "In Search of the Real Bill Gates."

Chapter 2: Discovering Computers

20. Quoted in Wallace and Erickson, *Hard Drive*, p. 19.
21. Quoted in Manes and Andrews, *Gates*, p. 27.
22. Gates, *The Road Ahead*, p. 1.
23. Quoted in Isaacson, "In Search of the Real Bill Gates."
24. Quoted in Wallace and Erickson, *Hard Drive*, p. 33.
25. Quoted in Isaacson, "In Search of the Real Bill Gates."
26. Quoted in Isaacson, "In Search of the Real Bill Gates."
27. Gates, *The Road Ahead*, pp. 13–14.
28. Quoted in Susan Lammers, *Programmers at Work*. Redmond, WA: Microsoft Press, 1986, p. 80.

Chapter 3: Writing BASIC

29. Quoted in Brenda Dalglish, "Genius at Work," *Maclean's*, May 11, 1992.
30. Quoted in Dalglish, "Genius at Work."
31. Quoted in Manes and Andrews, *Gates*, p. 58.
32. Quoted in Wallace and Erickson, *Hard Drive*, p. 57.
33. Gates, *The Road Ahead*, p. 39.
34. Quoted in Dalglish, "Genius at Work."
35. Quoted in Daniel Ichbiah and Susan L. Knepper, *The Making of Microsoft: How Bill Gates and His Team Created the World's Most Successful Software Company*. Rocklin, CA: Prima Publishing, 1991, p. 223.
36. Quoted in Isaacson, "In Search of the Real Bill Gates."
37. Quoted in Manes and Andrews, *Gates*, p. 63.
38. Quoted in Lammers, *Programmers at Work*, p. 79.
39. Quoted in Manes and Andrews, *Gates*, p. 71.

Chapter 4: Microsoft Is Born

40. Quoted in Wallace and Erickson, *Hard Drive*, p. 119.

41. Quoted in Lammers, *Programmers at Work*, p. 72.

42. Quoted in Ichbiah and Knepper, *The Making of Microsoft*, p. 30.

43. Gates, *The Road Ahead*, p. 44.

44. Gates, *The Road Ahead*, p. 18.

45. Quoted in Wallace and Erickson, *Hard Drive*, p. 97.

46. Quoted in Wallace and Erickson, *Hard Drive*, p. 115.

47. Manes and Andrews, *Gates*, p. 123.

Chapter 5: Return to the Northwest

48. Quoted in Manes and Andrews, *Gates*, p. 139.

49. Quoted in "Microsoft," *Inc.*, December 1984.

50. Quoted in Isaacson, "In Search of the Real Bill Gates."

51. Quoted in Isaacson, "In Search of the Real Bill Gates."

52. Quoted in Michael J. Miller, "Looking Beyond," *PC Magazine*, March 25, 1997.

53. Paul Carroll, *Big Blues*. New York: Crown, 1993, p. 9.

54. Quoted in Wallace and Erickson, *Hard Drive*, p. 169.

55. Moody, *I Sing the Body Electronic*, p. iv.

56. Gates, *The Road Ahead*, p. 48.

57. Stewart Alsop, "Differing Visions," *PC Magazine*, June 10, 1986.

58. Seabrook, "E-Mail from Bill," p. 58.

59. Quoted in Rensin, "Playboy Interview: Bill Gates."

60. Carroll, *Big Blues*, p. 35.

61. Quoted in Wallace and Erickson, *Hard Drive*, p. 204.

Chapter 6: Computer Wars

62. Quoted in Miller, "Looking Beyond."

63. Carroll, *Big Blues*, p. 2.

64. Moody, *I Sing the Body Electronic*, p. 56.

65. Quoted in Ichbiah and Knepper, *The Making of Microsoft*, p. 212.

66. Quoted in Wallace and Erickson, *Hard Drive*, p. 249.

67. Quoted in Manes and Andrews, *Gates*, p. 242.

68. Statford P. Sherman, "Microsoft's Drive to Dominate Software," *Fortune*, January 23, 1984.

69. Quoted in Rensin, "Playboy Interview: Bill Gates."
70. Quoted in Manes and Andrews, *Gates,* p. 225.
71. Quoted in "Microsoft."
72. Isaacson, "In Search of the Real Bill Gates."
73. Manes and Andrews, *Gates,* p. 251.

Chapter 7: New Location, New Power

74. Stross, *The Microsoft Way,* p. 17.
75. Quoted in Ken Auletta, "The Microsoft Provocateur," *New Yorker,* May 12, 1997.
76. Stross, *The Microsoft Way,* p. 56.
77. Quoted in Manes and Andrews, *Gates,* p. 322.
78. Quoted in Miller, "Looking Beyond."
79. Quoted in Wallace and Erickson, *Hard Drive,* pp. 375–76.
80. Quoted in Isaacson, "In Search of the Real Bill Gates."
81. Gates, *The Road Ahead,* p. 58.

Chapter 8: Balancing Family and Work

82. Quoted in Isaacson, "In Search of the Real Bill Gates."
83. Quoted in James Wallace, *Overdrive: Bill Gates and the Race to Control Cyberspace.* New York: Wiley, 1997, p. 55.
84. Quoted in Steven Levy, "Gates, Face to Face," *Newsweek,* December 2, 1996.
85. Gates, *The Road Ahead,* p. 226.
86. David Enna, "High-Tech Wizardry in Bill Gates' New Home Won't Become Common," *Charlotte Observer* (from Knight-Ridder/Tribune News Service), December 7, 1995.
87. Quoted in Wallace, *Overdrive,* p. 131.
88. Quoted in Rensin, "Playboy Interview: Bill Gates."
89. Gates, *The Road Ahead,* p. 91.
90. Stross, *The Microsoft Way,* p. 222.

Epilogue: Into the Future

91. Quoted in Rensin, "Playboy Interview: Bill Gates."
92. Quoted in Michelle Matassa Flores and Thomas W. Haines, "Microsoft, Apple Join Forces," *Seattle Times,* August 6, 1997.

93. Rensin, "Playboy Interview: Bill Gates."
94. Quoted in Isaacson, "In Search of the Real Bill Gates."
95. Quoted in Manes and Andrews, *Gates,* p. 440.
96. Quoted in Manes and Andrews, *Gates,* p. 416.
97. Quoted in Mike Brennan, "Internet Is Moving to Be Mainstream," *Detroit Free Press* (from Knight-Ridder/Tribune News Service), April 28, 1997.
98. Quoted in Miller, "Looking Beyond."
99. Quoted in Isaacson, "In Search of the Real Bill Gates."
100. Quoted in Rensin, "Playboy Interview: Bill Gates."
101. Quoted in Miller, "Looking Beyond."
102. Quoted in Moody, *I Sing the Body Electronic,* p. 69.

Important Dates in the Life of Bill Gates

1955
William Henry Gates III is born in Seattle, Washington, on October 28.

1967
Bill begins attending Lakeside School.

1968
Lakeside provides computer access for students.

1970
Lakeside Programmers Group is formed.

1973
Bill and Paul Allen form Traf-O-Data. Bill works for TRW; graduates from Lakeside and enters Harvard University.

1975
Bill and Paul write a version of BASIC for the Altair 8800, the first commercial microcomputer. Micro-Soft (now Microsoft) is formed in August, in Albuquerque, New Mexico.

1976
Microsoft establishes MS-BASIC with top computer manufacturers.

1978
Microsoft moves to Bellevue, Washington.

1980
Microsoft agrees to develop MS-BASIC and an operating system (DOS) for IBM.

1981
IBM PC is released, with MS-DOS 1.0. Bill sees a Macintosh pro-

totype, over two years before Apple begins to market the machine.

1982

Time magazine names the microcomputer as the "Man of the Year."

1983

Paul Allen leaves Microsoft because of illness.

1984

Apple releases the Macintosh. Microsoft becomes the first micro-computer software company to reach $100 million in sales.

1985

Microsoft Windows 1.0 is released to generally unfavorable reviews. Apple Computer files first of "look and feel" com-plaints against Microsoft.

1986

Microsoft moves to its campus in Redmond, Washington. The company goes public, and Bill becomes a multimillionaire.

1987

Bill becomes world's youngest billionaire.

1988

Bill buys land on Lake Washington for his high-tech house.

1990

Microsoft releases Windows 3.0 to great success. Microsoft and IBM undergo highly publicized "divorce." U.S. government probe into Microsoft's business practices begins.

1994

Bill marries Melinda French on New Year's Day. Mary Gates dies in June.

1995

Windows 95 becomes best-selling software product in history. Bill is named *Time* magazine's "Man of the Year."

1996

Jennifer Katharine Gates is born.

1997

Bill is named by *Forbes* magazine as richest individual in the world. Microsoft announces new alliance with Apple. Gates Library Foundation is announced.

Glossary

----

applications: Software, usually sold to the retail public, designed to perform specific tasks, such as word processing or drawing.

BASIC: Beginners' All-purpose Symbolic Instruction Code. An early programming language designed for use by nonprofessionals. The first version was developed in 1964.

bit: The smallest unit of information that a computer can store, digitally represented as a 1 or a 0.

bug: A glitch or malfunction in computer software or hardware. Dates from 1945, when a malfunction in an experimental computer at Harvard was found to have been due to a short circuit caused by a two-inch moth in the works.

bundling: The practice of selling an application and a computer together or two or more software applications together.

byte: Equals eight bits, or one character (such as a letter, number, or decimal point).

chip: The heart of a microprocessor, so called because it is built on a tiny chip of silicon.

CP/M: Control program/microcomputer, one of the first microcomputer operating systems.

CPU: Central processing unit; see microprocessor.

disk: Also diskette or floppy disk; the most commonly used storage medium for microcomputers; see hard disk.

DOS: Disk operating system. As MS-DOS, it is the most common operating system for IBM and compatible personal computers.

graphical user interface (GUI): The display of text and graphics on a computer screen, with images manipulated by a cursor or a mouse.

hack: To break into a computer system by devising a program that disables or circumvents the system's security measures.

hard disk: A magnetic storage medium that offers greater information storage capacity than floppy disks or diskettes.

kilobit (Kbit): A unit of measurement for computer memory; one Kbit equals 1,024 bits. A kilobyte (Kbyte) is 1,024 bytes.

mainframe: A large computer system, typically with high processing speed and storage capacity.

megabit (Mbit): A unit of measurement for computer memory; one megabit equals 1,024 kilobits. A megabyte (Mbyte) is 1,024 bytes.

microprocessor: The central processing unit or "brains" of a computer. It houses an integrated circuit (or chip) that uses electrical impulses to direct and perform the operations of the computer.

modem: A device for transmitting data from one computer to another over telecommunications lines. Early teletype terminals and microcomputers used "acoustic coupling" modems, to which telephone handsets were fit.

mouse: A device that is moved around to position a pointer on the computer screen at a desired location and perform tasks.

multitasking: Performing one or more operations simultaneously.

operating system: An essential program that controls all the basic functions of a computer.

RAM: Random access (volatile) memory. Refers to memory used to store information while a computer is operating.

ROM: Read-only (permanent) memory. Refers to memory that a computer can read but the user cannot manipulate.

window: On a GUI, a rectangular area of a computer screen in which a document or a running application is displayed. The concept of windows was developed at Xerox PARC, but its first commercial use was on the Macintosh computer.

word processor: An application program that enables a user to create, edit, reformat, and print documents.

For Further Reading

Aaron Boyd, *Smart Money*. Greensboro, NC: Morgan Reynolds, 1995. An introduction for young adults to Gates's life up to his marriage, this book is brief and entertaining, but sometimes inaccurate.

Ralph Zickgraf, *William Gates, from Whiz Kid to Software King*. Ada, OK: Garrett Educational Corporation, 1992. A short book for children about Gates, with an emphasis on his success as a businessman and entrepreneur.

Works Consulted

Books

Paul Carroll, *Big Blues.* New York: Crown, 1993. This well-written history explores how IBM made and lost a fortune in the 1980s.

Bill Gates, *The Road Ahead.* New York: Viking, 1995. This book about the future of computing and the information super-highway is written in a clear, nontechnical style, with significant input from journalist Peter Rinearson and Microsoft executive Nathan Myhrvold.

Daniel Ichbiah and Susan L. Knepper, *The Making of Microsoft: How Bill Gates and His Team Created the World's Most Successful Software Company.* Rocklin, CA: Prima Publishing, 1991. This is an English edition of a book by a French journalist. It has many inaccurate statements and unproven stories. As one of the first books to focus on Gates, however, it helped establish many of the legends that have built up around its subject.

Susan Lammers, *Programmers at Work.* Redmond, WA: Microsoft Press, 1986. A series of in-depth interviews with prominent computer programmers, including Bill Gates, this book is quite technical at times.

Stephen Manes and Paul Andrews, *Gates: How Microsoft's Mogul Reinvented an Industry—and Made Himself the Richest Man in America.* New York: Doubleday, 1993. Written by two respected Seattle-based journalists who specialize in high-tech issues, this is the most reliable biography so far of Gates. Often critical of its subject but generally even-handed, the book is heavily researched and extremely detailed.

Fred Moody, *I Sing the Body Electronic: A Year with Microsoft on the Multimedia Frontier.* New York: Viking, 1995. A book tracing a year in Microsoft's multimedia division, by a reporter for the *Seattle Weekly.* Contains excellent profiles of the workers who really make things happen in the company.

Randall E. Stross, *The Microsoft Way: The Real Story of How the Company Outsmarts Its Competition.* Reading, MA: Addison-Wesley, 1996. A book by a professor and business journalist, this work is largely sympathetic to Microsoft's business practices.

James Wallace, *Overdrive: Bill Gates and the Race to Control Cyberspace.* New York: Wiley, 1997. This sequel to *Hard Drive* focuses on Microsoft's efforts to gain market share on the Internet. Better organized than its predecessor, but similarly marred by the absence of notes and a bibliography.

James Wallace and Jim Erickson, *Hard Drive: Bill Gates and the Making of the Microsoft Empire.* New York: Wiley, 1992. This was the first full biography of Gates. The authors (reporters for the *Seattle Post-Intelligencer*) use a simple writing style that is easily accessible to nonexperts. The book is marred, however, by numerous factual errors; it also lacks footnotes, attributions, and a bibliography.

Periodicals

Stewart Alsop, "Differing Visions," *PC Magazine,* June 10, 1986. An article by a respected computer columnist contrasting two longtime rivals, Gary Kildall and Bill Gates.

Ken Auletta, "The Microsoft Provocateur," *New Yorker,* May 12, 1997. A lengthy profile of Gates's colleague Nathan Myhrvold.

Mike Brennan, "Internet Is Moving to Be Mainstream," *Detroit Free Press* (from Knight-Ridder/Tribune News Service), April 28, 1997. A brief interview with Bill Gates about the future of Microsoft and the Net.

Brenda Dalglish, "Genius at Work," *Maclean's,* May 11, 1992. A profile of Gates in a Canadian magazine.

David Enna, "High-Tech Wizardry in Bill Gates' New Home Won't Become Common," *Charlotte Observer* (from Knight-

Ridder/Tribune News Service), December 7, 1995. An opinion piece about high technology in homes.

Michelle Matassa Flores and Thomas W. Haines, "Microsoft, Apple Join Forces," *Seattle Times*, August 6, 1997. An article about Microsoft's move to consolidate forces with and support the faltering Apple company.

Michelle Matassa Flores, "What Does It All Mean?" *Seattle Times*, August 7, 1997. A follow-up analysis of the Apple-Microsoft alliance detailed by Flores and Haines.

Walter Isaacson, "In Search of the Real Bill Gates," *Time*, January 13, 1997. A lengthy, in-depth profile featuring interviews with many of Gates's friends, colleagues, and family members as well as Gates himself.

Letter from Bill Gates, *InfoWorld*, August 16, 1993.

Steven Levy, "Gates, Face to Face," *Newsweek*, December 2, 1996. A wide-ranging interview.

"Microsoft," *Inc.*, December 1984. A brief profile of the up-and-coming company shortly after Jon Shirley joined.

Michael J. Miller, "Looking Beyond," *PC Magazine*, March 25, 1997. A lengthy and sometimes highly technical interview with Bill Gates.

David Rensin, "Playboy Interview: Bill Gates," *Playboy*, July 1994. A far-ranging, nontechnical interview.

John Seabrook, "E-Mail from Bill," *New Yorker*, January 10, 1994. An account of the author's extensive e-mail correspondence with Gates, culminating in an in-person interview.

Statford P. Sherman, "Microsoft's Drive to Dominate Software," *Fortune*, January 23, 1984. An article focusing on the then-current bid to establish the dominance of Windows.

Website

www.glf.org A website devoted to information about Bill Gates's largest and most recent philanthropic effort, the Gates Library Foundation. It has links to many other sites, official and unofficial, about Gates.

Index

Picture Credits

About the Author

Adam Woog has written over a dozen books for adults and younger readers. He lives in his home town of Seattle, Washington, with his wife and young daughter.